On Core Mathematics

Grade 6

HOUGHTON MIFFLIN HARCOURT

Cover photo credit: David Stuckel/Alamy

Printed in the U.S.A.

ISBN 978-0-547-67498-8

17 18 19 20 2266 20

4500810081   ^ B C D E F G

Table of Contents

Ratios and Proportional Relationships

The Number System

Expressions and Equations

▶ **Apply and extend previous understandings of arithmetic to algebraic expressions.**

▶ **Reason about and solve one-variable equations and inequalities.**

▶ **Represent and analyze quantitative relationships between dependent and independent variables.**

Geometry

▶ Solve real-world and mathematical problems involving area, surface area, and volume.

Statistics and Probability

Statistics and Probability

▶ Develop understanding of statistical variability.

▶ Summarize and describe distributions.

Lesson 1

COMMON CORE STANDARD CC.6.RP.1
Lesson Objective: Model ratios.

Model Ratios

Daniel is growing tulips and daffodils in a pot.
For every 3 tulips he plants, he plants 1 daffodil.
How many daffodils will he plant if he plants
12 tulips?

Step 1 Make a model and write the ratio.
The ratio of tulips to daffodils is 3:1.

○ = 1 tulip
● = 1 daffodil

Step 2 Model the number of daffodils Daniel
will plant if he plants 6 tulips.

Step 3 Use the model and ratio to make a
table. The table shows that for every
3 tulips, there is 1 daffodil.

Tulips	3	6	9	12
Daffodils	1	2	3	4

Step 4 Find 12 tulips on the table. The
number of daffodils is 4.

Step 5 Write the new ratio.

The new ratio is 12:4.

So, if Daniel plants 12 tulips, he will plant 4 daffodils.

Write the ratio of triangles to squares.

1. _____ : _____

2. _____ : _____

Draw a model of the ratio.

3. 5:1

4. 3:4

Complete the table.

5. 1 table for every 5 students

Students	5		15	
Tables	1	2		4

6. 7 pencils for every 1 student

Students	1	2	3	
Pencils	7			28

Ratios and Proportional Relationships

Name _____

Model Ratios

Write the ratio of gray counters to white counters.

1.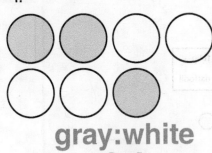

gray:white
3:4
_____

2.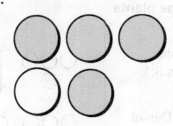

3.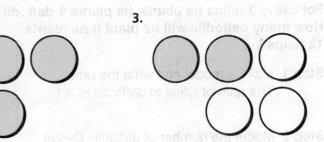

Draw a model of the ratio.

4. 5:1

5. 6:3

Use the ratio to complete the table.

6. Marc is assembling gift bags. For every 2 pencils he places in the bag, he uses 3 stickers. Complete the table to show the ratio of pencils to stickers.

Pencils	2	4	6	8
Stickers	3			

7. Singh is making a bracelet. She uses 5 blue beads for every 1 silver bead. Complete the table to show the ratio of blue beads to silver beads.

Blue	5	10		20
Silver	1		3	

Problem Solving

8. There are 4 quarts in 1 gallon. How many quarts are in 3 gallons?

_____

9. Martin mixes 1 cup lemonade with 4 cups cranberry juice to make his favorite drink. How much cranberry juice does he need if he uses 5 cups of lemonade?

_____

Name _____

COMMON CORE STANDARD CC.6.RP.1
Lesson Objective: Write ratios and rates.

Ratios and Rates

A **ratio** is a comparison of two numbers by division.
Ratios can compare parts of a whole or compare one part to the whole.
A **rate** is a ratio that compares two numbers that have different units.

> The picture shows a group of school supplies. One part is pencils.
> The other part is notebooks. Write the ratio of pencils to notebooks.
> Write the ratio using words, as a fraction, and with a colon.
>
> Write the number of pencils first, and then write the number of notebooks.
>
> | 12 to 4 | $\frac{12}{4}$ | 12:4 |
> |---|---|---|
> | number of pencils **to** number of notebooks | $\frac{\text{number of pencils}}{\text{number of notebooks}}$ | number of pencils **:** number of notebooks |
>
> You could also write a ratio comparing part to whole.
> Write the ratio of notebooks to school supplies, three ways.
>
> | 4 to 16 | $\frac{4}{16}$ | 4:16 |
> |---|---|---|
> | number of notebooks **to** number of school supplies | $\frac{\text{number of notebooks}}{\text{number of school supplies}}$ | number of notebooks **:** number of school supplies |

Write each ratio three ways.

1. Write the ratio of circles to squares.

_____ to _____ $\frac{\quad}{\quad}$ _____ : _____

2. Write the ratio of squares to shapes.

_____ to _____ $\frac{\quad}{\quad}$ _____ : _____

Ratios and Proportional Relationships

3

Ratios and Rates

Write the ratio in two different ways.

1. $\frac{4}{5}$

4 to 5

4:5

2. 16 to 3

_____

3. 9:13

_____

4. $\frac{2}{11}$

_____

5. 7:10

_____

6. $\frac{1}{6}$

_____

7. 22 to 4

_____

8. $\frac{15}{8}$

_____

9. There are 20 light bulbs in 5 packages. Complete the table to find the rate that gives the number of light bulbs in 3 packages. Write this rate in three different ways.

Light Bulbs		8		16	20
Packages	1	2	3	4	5

_____

_____

Problem Solving REAL WORLD

10. Gemma spends 4 hours each week playing soccer and 3 hours each week practicing her clarinet. Write the ratio of hours spent practicing clarinet to hours spent playing soccer three different ways.

_____

11. Randall bought 2 game controllers at Electronics Plus for $36. What is the unit rate for a game controller at Electronics Plus?

_____

Name _____

Lesson 3
COMMON CORE STANDARD CC.6.RP.2
Lesson Objective: Use unit rates to make comparisons.

Find Unit Rates

When comparing prices of items, the better buy is the item with a lower unit price.

Determine the better buy by comparing unit rates.

A 12-ounce box of Wheat-Os costs $4.08, and a 15-ounce box of Bran-Brans costs $5.40. Which brand is the better buy?

Step 1 Write a rate for each.

Wheat-Os		**Bran-Brans**

$$\frac{\$4.08}{12\,oz}$$ ⟵ Since you are looking for the lower cost per ounce, write cost over ounce. ⟶ $$\frac{\$5.40}{15\,oz}$$

Step 2 Write each rate as a unit rate.

$$\frac{\$4.08 \div 12}{12\,oz \div 12} = \frac{\$0.34}{1\,oz}$$

Divide the numerator and denominator by the number in the denominator.

$$\frac{\$5.40 \div 15}{15\,oz \div 15} = \frac{\$0.36}{1\,oz}$$

Step 3 Choose the brand that costs less.

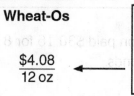 $\dfrac{\$0.34}{1\,oz}$ $\$0.34$ is less than $\$0.36$. $\dfrac{\$0.36}{1\,oz}$

So, Wheat-Os are the better buy.

Determine the better buy by comparing unit rates.

1. 20 pens for $1.60 or 25 pens for $2.25

    a. Write a rate for each.

    _____ and _____

    b. Write each rate as a unit rate.

    _____ and _____

    c. Which is the better buy?

    _____

2. 13 berries for $2.60 or 17 berries for $3.06

    a. Write a rate for each.

    _____ and _____

    b. Write each rate as a unit rate.

    _____ and _____

    c. Which is the better buy?

    _____

Ratios and Proportional Relationships

Name _____

Find Unit Rates

Write the rate as a fraction. Then find the unit rate.

1. A wheel rotates through 1,800° in 5 revolutions.

$$\frac{1{,}800°}{5 \text{ revolutions}}$$

$$\frac{1{,}800° \div 5}{5 \text{ revolutions} \div 5} = \frac{360°}{1 \text{ revolution}}$$

2. There are 312 cards in 6 decks of playing cards.

_____

3. Bana ran 18.6 miles of a marathon in 3 hours.

4. Cameron paid $30.16 for 8 pounds of almonds.

Compare unit rates.

5. An online game company offers a package that includes 2 games for $11.98. They also offer a package that includes 5 games for $24.95. Which package is a better deal?

6. At a track meet, Samma finished the 200-meter race in 25.98 seconds. Tom finished the 100-meter race in 12.54 seconds. Which runner ran at a faster average rate?

_____

7. Elmer Elementary School has 576 students and 24 teachers. Savoy Elementary School has 638 students and 29 teachers. Which school has the lower unit rate of students per teacher?

8. One cell phone company offers 500 minutes of talk time for $49.99. Another company offers 480 minutes for $44.99. Which company offers the better deal?

_____

Problem Solving  REAL WORLD

9. Sylvio's flight is scheduled to travel 1,792 miles in 3.5 hours. At what average rate will the plane have to travel to complete the trip on time?

10. Rachel bought 2 pounds of apples and 3 pounds of peaches for a total of $10.45. The apples and peaches cost the same amount per pound. What was the unit rate?

_____

Equivalent Ratios and Multiplication Tables

To find equivalent ratios, you can use a multiplication table or multiply by a form of 1.

Write two ratios equivalent to 10:14. Use a multiplication table.

Step 1 Find 10 and 14 in the same row.

Step 2 Look at the columns for 10 and 14.

Choose a number from each column. Make sure that the numbers you choose are in the same row.   5 and 7   30 and 42

Step 3 Write the new ratios.   5:7   30:42

×	1	2	3	4	5	6	7	8	9
1	1	2	3	4	5	6	7	8	9
2	2	4	6	8	10	12	14	16	18
3	3	6	9	12	15	18	21	24	27
4	4	8	12	16	20	24	28	32	36
5	5	10	15	20	25	30	35	40	45
6	6	12	18	24	30	36	42	48	54
7	7	14	21	28	35	42	49	56	63
8	8	16	24	32	40	48	56	64	72
9	9	18	27	36	45	54	63	72	81

Use multiplication or division.   **Multiply**   **Divide**

Step 1 To multiply or divide by a form of 1, multiply or divide the numerator and denominator by the same number. $\frac{10 \times 3}{14 \times 3} = \frac{30}{42}$ $\frac{10 \div 2}{14 \div 2} = \frac{5}{7}$

Step 2 Write the new ratios. $\frac{30}{42}$ $\frac{5}{7}$

Solve.

1. Write a ratio that is equivalent to 6:16.

  a. Find 6 and 16 in the same row.

  b. Choose a pair of numbers from a different row, in the same _____ and _____ columns as 6 and 16.

  c. Write the equivalent ratio.   6:16 = _____ : _____

×	1	2	3	4	5	6	7	8	9
1	1	2	3	4	5	6	7	8	9
2	2	4	6	8	10	12	14	16	18
3	3	6	9	12	15	18	21	24	27
4	4	8	12	16	20	24	28	32	36
5	5	10	15	20	25	30	35	40	45
6	6	12	18	24	30	36	42	48	54
7	7	14	21	28	35	42	49	56	63
8	8	16	24	32	40	48	56	64	72
9	9	18	27	36	45	54	63	72	81

2. Write two ratios equivalent to $\frac{5}{9}$.   **3.** Write two ratios equivalent to $\frac{8}{6}$.

Equivalent Ratios and Multiplication Tables

Write two equivalent ratios.

1. Use a multiplication table to write two ratios that are equivalent to $\frac{5}{3}$.

$$\frac{5}{3} = \frac{10}{6}, \frac{15}{9}$$

2.

6			
7			

3.

3		
2		

4.

9		
2		

5.

7		
10		

6. $\frac{4}{5}$

7. $\frac{1}{9}$

8. $\frac{6}{8}$

9. $\frac{11}{1}$

_____   _____   _____

Determine whether the ratios are equivalent.

10. $\frac{2}{3}$ and $\frac{5}{6}$

11. $\frac{5}{10}$ and $\frac{1}{6}$

12. $\frac{8}{3}$ and $\frac{32}{12}$

13. $\frac{9}{12}$ and $\frac{3}{4}$

_____   _____   _____

Problem Solving REAL WORLD

14. Tristan uses 7 stars and 9 diamonds to make a design. Write two ratios that are equivalent to $\frac{7}{9}$.

15. There are 12 girls and 16 boys in Javier's math class. There are 26 girls and 14 boys in Javier's choir class. Is the ratio of girls to boys in the two classes equivalent? Explain.

_____   _____

Name _____

Lesson 5
COMMON CORE STANDARD CC.6.RP.3a
Lesson Objective: Solve problems involving
ratios by using the strategy *find a pattern*.

Problem Solving • Use Tables to Compare Ratios

Use tables of equivalent ratios to solve the problem.

Kevin's cookie recipe uses a ratio of 4 parts flour to 2 parts sugar.
Anna's recipe uses 5 parts flour to 3 parts sugar. Could their recipes
make the same cookies?

Read the Problem	Solve the Problem
What do I need to find? I need to find out if the ratio of _____ to _____ in Kevin's recipe is equivalent to the ratio in _____.	Make a table of equivalent ratios for each recipe. **Kevin's Recipe** <table><tr><td>Flour</td><td>4</td><td>8</td><td>12</td><td>16</td><td>20</td></tr><tr><td>Sugar</td><td>2</td><td>4</td><td>6</td><td>8</td><td>10</td></tr></table> **Anna's Recipe** <table><tr><td>Flour</td><td>5</td><td>10</td><td>15</td><td>20</td><td>25</td></tr><tr><td>Sugar</td><td>3</td><td>6</td><td>9</td><td>12</td><td>15</td></tr></table>
What information do I need to use? I will use the _____ of _____ to _____.	Find an amount of flour that is in both tables. _____ Write the ratio for Kevin's recipe. $\frac{20}{\boxed{}}$
How will I use the information? I will make _____ to compare the _____.	Write the ratio for Anna's recipe. $\frac{20}{\boxed{}}$ Are the ratios the same? _____ So, their recipes _____ make the same cookies.

1. Sherona takes a 6-minute break after every 24 minutes of study. Benedict takes an 8-minute break after every 32 minutes of study. Are their ratios of study time to break time equivalent?

2. Micah buys 10 pens for every 2 pencils. Rachel buys 12 pens for every 3 pencils. Are their ratios of pens to pencils bought equivalent?

Ratios and Proportional Relationships

9

Name _____

Problem Solving • Use Tables to Compare Ratios

Read each problem and solve.

1. Sarah asked some friends about their favorite colors. She found that 4 out of 6 people prefer blue, and 8 out of 12 people prefer green. Is the ratio of friends who chose blue to the total asked equivalent to the ratio of friends who chose green to the total asked?

Blue				
Friends who chose blue	4	8	12	16
Total asked	6	12	18	24

Green				
Friends who chose green	8	16	24	32
Total asked	12	24	36	48

Yes, $\frac{4}{6}$ is equivalent to $\frac{8}{12}$.

2. Lisa and Tim make necklaces. Lisa uses 5 red beads for every 3 yellow beads. Tim uses 9 red beads for every 6 yellow beads. Is the ratio of red beads to yellow beads in Lisa's necklace equivalent to the ratio in Tim's necklace?

3. Mitch scored 4 out of 5 on a quiz. Demetri scored 8 out of 10 on a quiz. Did Mitch and Demetri get equivalent scores?

4. Chandra ordered 10 chicken nuggets and ate 7 of them. Raul ordered 15 chicken nuggets and ate 12 of them. Is Chandra's ratio of nuggets ordered to nuggets eaten equivalent to Raul's ratio of nuggets ordered to nuggets eaten?

Name _____

Lesson 6
COMMON CORE STANDARD CC.6.RP.3a
Lesson Objective: Use tables to solve problems involving equivalent ratios.

Algebra • Use Equivalent Ratios

You can find equivalent ratios by using a table or by multiplying or dividing the numerator and denominator by the same number.

Kate reads 5 chapters in 2 hours. At this rate, how many chapters will she read in 6 hours?

Step 1 Make a table of equivalent ratios.

$$5 \cdot 2 \quad 5 \cdot 3$$

Chapters read	5	10	15
Time (hours)	2	4	6

$$2 \cdot 2 \quad 2 \cdot 3$$

Step 2 Find 6 hours in the table. Find the number of chapters that goes with 6 hours: 15

Step 3 Write the new ratio: $\frac{15}{6}$

The ratios $\frac{5}{2}$ and $\frac{15}{6}$ are equivalent ratios. So, Kate will read 15 chapters in 6 hours.

Julian runs 10 kilometers in 60 minutes. At this pace, how many kilometers can he run in 30 minutes?

Step 1 Write equivalent ratios with a missing value.

$$\frac{10}{60} = \frac{\blacksquare}{30}$$

Step 2 Divide the numerator and denominator by 2 to write the ratios using a common denominator.

$$\frac{10 \div 2}{60 \div 2} = \frac{\blacksquare}{30}$$

The denominators are the same, so the numerators are equal to each other.

$$\frac{5}{30} = \frac{\blacksquare}{30} \rightarrow \blacksquare = 5$$

So, Julian can run 5 kilometers in 30 minutes.

Use equivalent ratios to find the unknown value.

1. $\frac{4}{5} = \dfrac{\boxed{}}{20}$

$$4 \cdot 2 \quad 4 \cdot 3 \quad 4 \cdot 4$$

4		12	
5	10		20

$$5 \cdot 2 \quad 5 \cdot 3 \quad 5 \cdot 4$$

2. $\dfrac{\boxed{}}{12} = \frac{2}{3}$

$$2 \cdot 2 \quad 2 \cdot 3 \quad 2 \cdot 4$$

2			
3			12

$$3 \cdot 2 \quad 3 \cdot 3 \quad 3 \cdot 4$$

3. $\frac{24}{27} = \dfrac{\boxed{}}{9}$

4. $\frac{3}{7} = \dfrac{9}{\boxed{}}$

5. $\frac{8}{10} = \dfrac{\boxed{}}{5}$

6. $\frac{30}{45} = \dfrac{6}{\boxed{}}$

Name _____

Use Equivalent Ratios

Use equivalent ratios to find the unknown value.

1. $\dfrac{4}{10} = \dfrac{\blacksquare}{40}$

$\dfrac{4 \times 4}{10 \times 4} = \dfrac{\blacksquare}{40}$

$\dfrac{16}{40} = \dfrac{\blacksquare}{40}$

$\blacksquare = 16$

2. $\dfrac{3}{24} = \dfrac{33}{\blacksquare}$

3. $\dfrac{7}{\blacksquare} = \dfrac{21}{27}$

4. $\dfrac{\blacksquare}{9} = \dfrac{12}{54}$

5. $\dfrac{3}{2} = \dfrac{12}{\blacksquare}$

6. $\dfrac{4}{5} = \dfrac{\blacksquare}{40}$

7. $\dfrac{\blacksquare}{2} = \dfrac{45}{30}$

8. $\dfrac{8}{\blacksquare} = \dfrac{16}{18}$

9. $\dfrac{45}{\blacksquare} = \dfrac{5}{6}$

10. $\dfrac{\blacksquare}{18} = \dfrac{7}{3}$

11. $\dfrac{36}{50} = \dfrac{18}{\blacksquare}$

12. $\dfrac{32}{12} = \dfrac{\blacksquare}{3}$

Problem Solving

13. Honeybees produce 7 pounds of honey for every 1 pound of beeswax they produce. Use equivalent ratios to find how many pounds of honey are produced when 25 pounds of beeswax are produced.

14. A 3-ounce serving of tuna provides 21 grams of protein. Use equivalent ratios to find how many grams of protein are in 9 ounces of tuna.

Name _____

Algebra • Equivalent Ratios and Graphs

Jake collects 12 new coins each year. Use equivalent ratios to graph the growth of his coin collection over time.

Step 1 Write an ordered pair for the first year. Let the *x*-coordinate represent the number of years: 1. Let the *y*-coordinate represent the number of coins: 12.

Ordered pair: (1, 12)

Coins	12	24	36	48	60
Year	1	2	3	4	5

Step 2 Make a table of equivalent ratios.

Step 3 Write ordered pairs for the values in the table.

(1, 12), (2, 24), (3, 36), (4, 48), (5, 60)

Step 4 Label the *x*-axis and *y*-axis.

Step 5 Graph the ordered pairs as points.

The point (1, 12) represents the year Jake started his collection. It shows that he had 12 coins after 1 year.

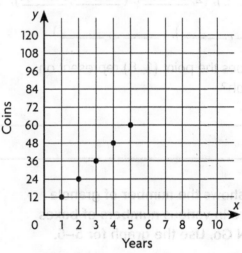

Use the graph for 1–5.

1. Helen walks at a rate of 3 miles in 1 hour. Write an ordered pair. Let the *y*-coordinate represent miles and the *x*-coordinate represent hours. (___ , ___)

2. Complete the table of equivalent ratios.

Miles	3			12	
Hours			3		5

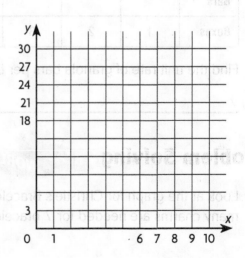

3. Write ordered pairs for the values in the table.

(___ , ___), (___ , ___), (___ , ___), (___ , ___), (___ , ___)

4. Label the graph. Graph the ordered pairs.

5. What does the point (2, 6) represent on the graph?

Ratios and Proportional Relationships

13

Name _____

Equivalent Ratios and Graphs

Christie makes bracelets. She uses 8 charms for each bracelet.
Use this information for 1–4.

1. Complete the table of equivalent ratios for the first 5 bracelets.

Charms	8	16	24	32	40
Bracelets	1	2	3	4	5

2. Write ordered pairs, letting the x-coordinate represent the number of bracelets and the y-coordinate represent the number of charms.

(1, _8_), (2, _16_), (____ , ____),

(____ , ____), (____ , ____)

4. What does the point (1, 8) represent on the graph?

_____

_____

3. Use the ordered pairs to graph the charms and bracelets.

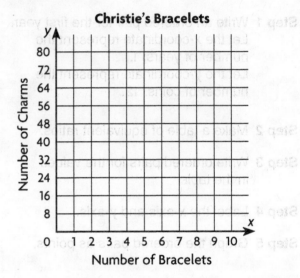

Christie's Bracelets

The graph shows the number of granola bars that are in various numbers of boxes of Crunch N Go. Use the graph for 5–6.

5. Complete the table of equivalent ratios.

Bars				
Boxes	1	2	3	4

6. Find the unit rate of granola bars per box.

_____

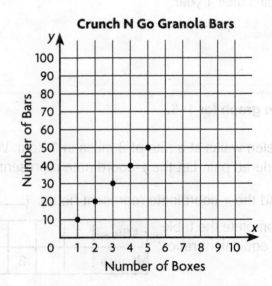

Crunch N Go Granola Bars

Problem Solving REAL WORLD

7. Look at the graph for Christie's Bracelets. How many charms are needed for 7 bracelets?

_____

8. Look at the graph for Crunch N Go Granola Bars. Stefan needs to buy 90 granola bars. How many boxes must he buy?

_____

Algebra • Use Unit Rates

You can find equivalent ratios by first finding a unit rate.

Marcia makes bracelets to sell at craft fairs. She sold 14 bracelets for $154. How much could she expect to earn if she sells 25 bracelets?

Step 1 Write equivalent ratios.

$$\frac{\text{money} \rightarrow}{\text{bracelets} \rightarrow} \frac{\$154}{14} = \frac{\blacksquare}{25} \begin{array}{l}\leftarrow \text{money} \\ \leftarrow \text{bracelets}\end{array}$$

Step 2 Since 25 is not a multiple of 14, use the known ratio to find a unit rate.

$$\frac{\$154 \div \boxed{14}}{14 \div 14} = \frac{\blacksquare}{25}$$

$$\frac{\$\boxed{11}}{1} = \frac{\blacksquare}{25}$$

> Marcia earns $11 per bracelet.

Step 3 Write an equivalent ratio by multiplying the unit rate's numerator and denominator by the same value. Since 1 · 25 = 25, multiply by 25 over 25.

$$\frac{\$11 \cdot \boxed{25}}{1 \cdot \boxed{25}} = \frac{\blacksquare}{25}$$

Step 4 Since the denominators are equal, the numerators are also equal.

$$\frac{\boxed{\$275}}{25} = \frac{\blacksquare}{25}$$

So, Marcia would earn $275 if she sells 25 bracelets.

Use a unit rate to find the unknown value.

1. $\dfrac{120}{20} = \dfrac{300}{\blacksquare}$

   a. Find the unit rate: $\dfrac{120 \div \boxed{}}{20 \div 20} = \dfrac{300}{\blacksquare}$

   b. $\dfrac{\boxed{}}{1} = \dfrac{300}{\blacksquare}$

   c. $\dfrac{6 \cdot 50}{1 \cdot \boxed{}} = \dfrac{300}{\blacksquare}$

   d. $\blacksquare$ = _____

2. $\dfrac{\blacksquare}{100} = \dfrac{90}{15}$

   $\blacksquare$ = _____

3. $\dfrac{90}{\blacksquare} = \dfrac{44}{22}$

   $\blacksquare$ = _____

4. $\dfrac{45}{10} = \dfrac{\blacksquare}{54}$

   $\blacksquare$ = _____

Use Unit Rates

Use a unit rate to find the unknown value.

1. $\dfrac{34}{17} = \dfrac{\blacksquare}{7}$

$\dfrac{34 \div 17}{17 \div 17} = \dfrac{\blacksquare}{7}$

$\dfrac{2}{1} = \dfrac{\blacksquare}{7}$

$\dfrac{2 \times 7}{1 \times 7} = \dfrac{\blacksquare}{7}$

$\dfrac{14}{7} = \dfrac{\blacksquare}{7}$

$\blacksquare = 14$

2. $\dfrac{16}{32} = \dfrac{\blacksquare}{14}$

3. $\dfrac{18}{\blacksquare} = \dfrac{21}{7}$

4. $\dfrac{\blacksquare}{16} = \dfrac{3}{12}$

Draw a bar model to find the unknown value.

5. $\dfrac{15}{45} = \dfrac{6}{\blacksquare}$

_____

6. $\dfrac{3}{6} = \dfrac{\blacksquare}{7}$

_____

7. $\dfrac{\blacksquare}{6} = \dfrac{6}{9}$

_____

8. $\dfrac{7}{\blacksquare} = \dfrac{2}{10}$

Problem Solving  REAL WORLD

9. To stay properly hydrated, a person should drink 32 fluid ounces of water for every 60 minutes of exercise. How much water should Damon drink if he rides his bike for 135 minutes?

10. Lillianne made 6 out of every 10 baskets she attempted during basketball practice. If she attempted to make 25 baskets, how many did she make?

_____

_____

Name _____

Lesson 9

COMMON CORE STANDARD CC.6.RP.3c

Lesson Objective: Use a model to show a percent as a rate per 100.

Model Percents

A **percent** is a ratio that compares a number to 100. It represents part of a whole.

Model 54% on the 10-by-10 grid. Then write the percent as a ratio.

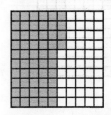

Step 1 The grid represents 1 whole. It has 100 equal parts. To show 54%, shade 54 of the 100 equal parts.

Step 2 A ratio can be written as a fraction. Write the number of shaded parts, 54, in the numerator. Write the total number of parts in the whole, 100, in the denominator.

shaded ⟶ $\dfrac{54}{100}$
total ⟶

So, 54% is 54 out of 100 squares shaded, or $\dfrac{54}{100}$.

Model the percent and write it as a ratio.

1. 19%

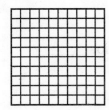

ratio: _____

2. 80%

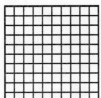

ratio: _____

3. 66%

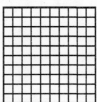

ratio: _____

4. 3%

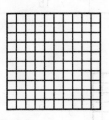

ratio: _____

5. 31%

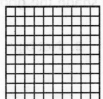

ratio: _____

6. 25%

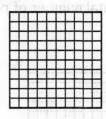

ratio: _____

Ratios and Proportional Relationships

Model Percents

Write a ratio and a percent to represent the shaded part.

1.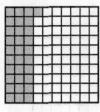

ratio: $\dfrac{31}{100}$ percent: **31%**

2.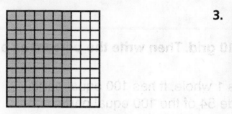

ratio: _____   percent: _____

3.

ratio: _____   percent: _____

Model the percent and write it as a ratio.

4. 97%

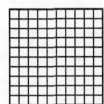

ratio: _____

5. 24%

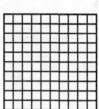

ratio: _____

6. 50%

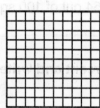

ratio: _____

Problem Solving REAL WORLD

The table shows the pen colors sold at the school supply store one week. Write the ratio comparing the number of the given color sold to the total number of pens sold. Then shade the grid.

Pens Sold	
Color	Number
Blue	36
Black	49
Red	15

7. Black

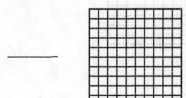

_____

8. Not blue

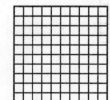

_____

Write Percents as Fractions and Decimals

You can write a percent as a decimal and a fraction.

Write 140% as a decimal and as a fraction in simplest form.

Step 1 Write 140% as a decimal by dividing 140 by 100. This results in the decimal point moving two places to the left.

$140\% = 140 = 1.40$

Step 2 Write 1.40 as a fraction by writing the 1 as a whole number and the decimal as a fraction. The 40 after the decimal point represents 40 hundredths. So, write 40 in the numerator and 100 in the denominator.

$1.40 = 1\dfrac{40}{100}$

Step 3 Simplify.

$1\dfrac{40}{100} = 1\dfrac{2}{5}$

So, $140\% = 1.40 = 1\dfrac{2}{5}$.

Write the percent as a decimal and as a fraction in simplest form.

1. 75%

2. 44%

3. 128%

4. 5%

_____ _____ _____ _____

5. 464%

6. 38%

7. 7%

8. 0.6%

_____ _____ _____ _____

9. 234%

10. 0.9%

11. 72%

12. 8%

_____ _____ _____ _____

Write Percents as Fractions and Decimals

Write the percent as a fraction or mixed number.

1. 44%

$$44\% = \frac{44}{100}$$
$$= \frac{11}{25}$$

2. 32%

3. 116%

4. 250%

5. 0.3%

6. 0.4%

7. 1.5%

8. 12.5%

Write the percent as a decimal.

9. 63%

10. 90%

11. 110%

12. 8%

13. 42.15%

14. 2.5%

15. 0.1%

16. 22.1%

Problem Solving  REAL WORLD

17. An online bookstore sells 0.8% of its books to foreign customers. What fraction of the books are sold to foreign customers?

18. In Mr. Klein's class, 40% of the students are boys. What decimal represents the portion of the students that are girls?

Name _____

Lesson 11
COMMON CORE STANDARD CC.6.RP.3c
Lesson Objective: Write fractions and decimals as percents.

Write Fractions and Decimals as Percents

You can write fractions and decimals as percents.

To write a decimal as a percent, multiply the decimal by 100 and write the percent symbol.

0.073 = 7.3% ⟵ To multiply by 100, move the decimal point two places to the right.

To write a fraction as a percent, divide the numerator by the denominator. Then write the decimal as a percent.

To write $\frac{3}{8}$ as a percent, first divide 3 by 8.

```
    0.375
8)3.000
  −24↓
    60
   −56↓
     40
    −40
      0
```

So, $\frac{3}{8}$ = 0.375.

0.375 = 37.5% ⟵ To write 0.375 as a percent, multiply by 100 and write the percent symbol.

Write the decimal or fraction as a percent.

1. 0.45

2. 0.6

3. 2.34

4. $\frac{7}{8}$

5. $\frac{19}{50}$

6. 0.03

7. $1\frac{11}{16}$

8. $\frac{51}{10}$

Write Fractions and Decimals as Percents

Write the fraction or decimal as a percent.

1. $\frac{7}{20}$ **2.** $\frac{3}{50}$ **3.** $\frac{1}{25}$ **4.** $\frac{5}{5}$

$$\frac{7}{20} = \frac{7 \times 5}{20 \times 5}$$
$$= \frac{35}{100} = 35\%$$

5. 0.622   **6.** 0.303   **7.** 0.06   **8.** 2.45

Write the number in two other forms (fraction, decimal, or percent).

9. $\frac{19}{20}$ **10.** $\frac{9}{16}$ **11.** 0.4   **12.** 0.22

Problem Solving REAL WORLD

13. According to the U.S. Census Bureau, $\frac{3}{25}$ of all adults in the United States visited a zoo in 2007. What percent of all adults in the United States visited a zoo in 2007?

14. A bag contains red and blue marbles. Given that $\frac{17}{20}$ of the marbles are red, what percent of the marbles are blue?

Percent of a Quantity

You can use ratios to write a percent of a quantity.

Find 0.9% of 30.

Step 1 Write the percent as a rate per 100. $0.9\% = \dfrac{0.9}{100}$

Step 2 Multiply by a fraction equivalent to 1 to get a whole number in the numerator. $\dfrac{0.9}{100} \times \dfrac{10}{10} = \dfrac{9}{1,000}$

Step 3 Write the multiplication problem. $\dfrac{9}{1,000} \times 30$

Step 4 Multiply. $\dfrac{9}{1,000} \times 30 = \dfrac{27}{100} = 0.27$

So, 0.9% of 30 is 0.27.

Find the percent of the quantity.

1. 8% of 90

2. 20% of 80

3. 95% of 340

4. 33% of 28

_____ _____ _____ _____

5. 200% of 8.5

6. 125% of 70

7. 0.25% of 120

8. 0.4% of 50

_____ _____ _____ _____

9. 45% of 70

10. 155% of 30

11. 75% of 124

12. 0.8% of 1,000

_____ _____ _____ _____

13. James correctly answered 85% of the 60 problems on his math test. How many questions did James answer correctly?

14. A basketball player missed 25% of her 52 free throws. How many free throws did the basketball player make?

_____ _____

Percent of a Quantity

Find the percent of the quantity.

1. 60% of 140

$$60\% = \frac{60}{100}$$

$$\frac{60}{100} \times 140$$
$$= 84$$

2. 55% of 600

_____

3. 4% of 50

_____

4. 50% of 82

_____

5. 10% of 2,350

_____

6. 80% of 40

_____

7. 160% of 30

_____

8. 250% of 2

_____

9. 105% of 260

_____

10. 0.5% of 12

_____

11. 40% of 16.5

_____

12. 75% of 8.4

_____

Problem Solving  REAL WORLD

13. The recommended daily amount of vitamin C for children 9 to 13 years old is 45 mg. A serving of a juice drink contains 60% of the recommended amount. How much vitamin C does the juice drink contain?

_____

14. During a 60-minute television program, 25% of the time is used for commercials and 5% of the time is used for the opening and closing credits. How many minutes remain for the program itself?

_____

Problem Solving • Percents

Use a model to solve the percent problem.

Lucia is driving to visit her parents, who live 240 miles away from her house. She has already driven 15% of the distance. How many miles does she still have to drive?

Read the Problem	Solve the Problem
What do I need to find? _____ _____ _____	Use a bar model to help. Draw a bar to represent the total distance. Then draw a bar that represents the distance driven plus the distance left.
What information do I need to use? _____ _____ _____ _____	100% total distance [240 miles] distance driven [?] [- - - -] 15% The model shows that 100% = _____ miles,
How will I use the information? _____ _____ _____ _____	so 1% of 240 = $\frac{240}{100}$ = _____ miles. 15% of 240 = 15 × _____ = _____ So, Lucia has already driven _____ miles. She still has to drive 240 − _____ = _____ miles.

1. At a deli, 56 sandwiches were sold during lunchtime. Twenty-five percent of the sandwiches sold were tuna salad sandwiches. How many of the sandwiches sold were not tuna salad?

_____

2. Mr. Brown bought a TV for $450. He has already paid 60% of the purchase price. How much has he already paid and how much does he have left to pay?

_____

Ratios and Proportional Relationships

Problem Solving • Percents

Read each problem and solve.

1. On Saturday, a souvenir shop had
   125 customers. Sixty-four percent of
   the customers paid with a credit card.
   The other customers paid with cash.
   How many customers paid with cash?

   $$1\% \text{ of } 125 = \frac{125}{100} = 1.25$$

   $$64\% \text{ of } 125 = 64 \times 1.25 = 80$$

   $$125 - 80 = 45 \text{ customers}$$

2. A carpenter has a wooden stick that is
   84 centimeters long. She cuts off 25% from the end
   of the stick. Then she cuts the remaining stick into
   6 equal pieces. What is the length of each piece?

   _____

3. Mike has $136 to spend at the amusement park.
   He spends 25% of that money on his ticket into the
   park. How much does Mike have left to spend?

   _____

4. A car dealership has 240 cars in the parking lot
   and 17.5% of them are red. Of the other 6 colors in
   the lot, each color has the same number of cars. If
   one of the colors is black, how many black cars are
   in the lot?

   _____

5. The utilities bill for the Millers' home in April was
   $132. Forty-two percent of the bill was for gas,
   and the rest was for electricity. How much did the
   Millers pay for gas, and how much did they pay for
   electricity?

   _____

6. Andy's total bill for lunch is $20. The cost of the
   drink is 15% of the total bill and the rest is the cost
   of the food. What percent of the total bill did Andy's
   food cost? What was the cost of his food?

   _____

Name _____

Lesson 14

COMMON CORE STANDARD CC.6.RP.3c

Lesson Objective: Find the whole given a part and the percent.

Find the Whole From a Percent

You can use equivalent ratios to find the whole, given a part and the percent.

---

54 is 60% of what number?

Step 1 Write the relationship among the percent, part, and whole. The percent is 60%. The part is 54. The whole is unknown.

$$\text{percent} = \frac{\text{part}}{\text{whole}}$$

$$60\% = \frac{54}{\blacksquare}$$

Step 2 Write the percent as a ratio.

$$\frac{60}{100} = \frac{54}{\blacksquare}$$

Step 3 Simplify the known ratio.

- Find the greatest common factor (GCF) of the numerator and denominator.

$$60 = 2 \times 2 \times 3 \times 5$$
$$100 = 2 \times 2 \times 5 \times 5 \longrightarrow GCF = 2 \times 2 \times 5 = 20$$

- Divide both the numerator and denominator by the GCF.

$$\frac{60 \div 20}{100 \div 20} = \frac{54}{\blacksquare}$$

$$\frac{3}{5} = \frac{54}{\blacksquare}$$

Step 4 Write an equivalent ratio.

- Look at the numerators. *Think:* $3 \times 18 = 54$

- Multiply the denominator by 18 to find the whole.

$$\frac{3 \times 18}{5 \times 18} = \frac{54}{\blacksquare}$$

So, 54 is 60% of 90.

$$\frac{54}{90} = \frac{54}{\blacksquare}$$

Find the unknown value.

1. 12 is 40% of _____

2. 15 is 25% of _____

3. 24 is 20% of _____

4. 36 is 50% of _____

5. 4 is 80% of _____

6. 12 is 15% of _____

7. 36 is 90% of _____

8. 12 is 75% of _____

9. 27 is 30% of _____

Ratios and Proportional Relationships

Name _____

Lesson 14

CC.6.RP.3c

Find the Whole From a Percent

Find the unknown value.

1. 9 is 15% of ___60___

$$\frac{15}{100} = \frac{9}{\boxed{}}$$

$$\frac{15 \div 5}{100 \div 5} = \frac{3 \times 3}{20 \times 3} = \frac{9}{60}$$

2. 54 is 75% of _____

3. 12 is 2% of _____

4. 18 is 50% of _____

5. 16 is 40% of _____

6. 56 is 28% of _____

7. 5 is 10% of _____

8. 24 is 16% of _____

9. 15 is 25% of _____

10. 11 is 44% of _____

11. 19 is 95% of _____

12. 10 is 20% of _____

Problem Solving REAL WORLD

13. Michaela is hiking on a weekend camping trip. She has walked 6 miles so far. This is 30% of the total distance. What is the total number of miles she will walk?

14. A customer placed an order with a bakery for cupcakes. The baker has completed 37.5% of the order after baking 81 cupcakes. How many cupcakes did the customer order?

_____

_____

28

Convert Units of Length

To convert a unit of measure, multiply by a conversion factor. A **conversion factor** is a rate in which the two quantities are equal, but are expressed in different units.

Convert to the given unit. 2,112 ft = _____ mi

Customary Units of Length
1 foot (ft) = 12 inches (in.)
1 yard (yd) = 36 inches
1 yard = 3 feet
1 mile (mi) = 5,280 feet
1 mile = 1,760 yards

Step 1 Choose a conversion factor.

1 mile = 5,280 feet, so use the conversion factor $\frac{1 \text{ mile}}{5,280 \text{ feet}}$.

Step 2 Multiply by the conversion factor.

$2,112 \text{ ft} \times \frac{1 \text{ mi}}{5,280 \text{ ft}} = \frac{2,112 \text{ ft}}{1} \times \frac{1 \text{ mi}}{5,280 \text{ ft}} = \frac{2,112}{5,280} \text{ mi} = \frac{2}{5} \text{ mi}$

So, $2,112 \text{ ft} = \frac{2}{5}$ mi.

When converting metric units, move the decimal point to multiply or divide by a power of ten.

14 dm = _____ hm

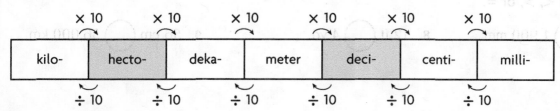

Step 1 Start at the given unit.

Step 2 Move to the unit you are converting to.

Step 3 Move the decimal point that same number of spaces in the same direction. Fill any empty place-value positions with zeros.

So, 14 dm = 0.014 hm.

Convert to the given unit.

1. 4.5 miles = _____ yards

2. 0.8 hectometers = _____ millimeters

3. 48 inches = _____ feet

4. 45 centimeters = _____ dekameters

Convert Units of Length

Convert to the given unit.

1. 42 ft = _____ yd

2. 2,350 m = _____ km

3. 18 ft = _____ in.

conversion factor: $\dfrac{1 \text{ yd}}{3 \text{ ft}}$

$42 \text{ ft} \times \dfrac{1 \text{ yd}}{3 \text{ ft}}$

$42 \text{ ft} = 14 \text{ yd}$

4. 289 m = _____ dm

5. 5 mi = _____ yd

6. 35 mm = _____ cm

Compare. Write <, >, or =.

7. 1.9 dm ◯ 1,900 mm

8. 12 ft ◯ 4 yd

9. 56 cm ◯ 56,000 km

10. 98 in. ◯ 8 ft

11. 64 cm ◯ 630 mm

12. 2 mi ◯ 10,560 ft

Problem Solving  REAL WORLD

13. The giant swallowtail is the largest butterfly in the United States. Its wingspan can be as large as 16 centimeters. What is the maximum wingspan in millimeters?

14. The 102nd floor of the Sears Tower in Chicago is the highest occupied floor. It is 1,431 feet above the ground. How many yards above the ground is the 102nd floor?

_____

_____

Name _____

Convert Units of Capacity

Capacity is the measure of the amount that a container can hold. When converting customary units, multiply the initial measurement by a conversion factor.

Convert to the given unit. 35 c = _____ qt

Step 1 Choose a conversion factor.

1 quart = 4 cups, so use the conversion factor $\frac{1\ quart}{4\ cups}$.

Step 2 Multiply by the conversion factor.

$35\ c \times \frac{1\ qt}{4\ c} = \frac{35\ c}{1} \times \frac{1\ qt}{4\ c} = \frac{35}{4}$ qt $= 8\frac{3}{4}$ qt

You can rename the fractional part using the smaller unit.

Customary Units of Capacity
8 fluid ounces (fl oz) = 1 cup (c)
2 cups = 1 pint (pt)
2 pints = 1 quart (qt)
4 cups = 1 quart
4 quarts = 1 gallon (gal)

$8\frac{3}{4}$ quarts = 8 quarts, 3 cups

So, 35 c = $8\frac{3}{4}$ qt, or 8 qt, 3 c.

When converting metric units, move the decimal point to multiply or divide by a power of ten.

26 cL = _____ hL

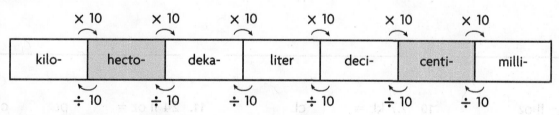

Step 1 Start at the given unit.

Step 2 Move to the unit you are converting to.

Step 3 Move the decimal point that same number of spaces in the same direction. Fill any empty place-value positions with zeros.

So, 26 cL = 0.0026 hL.

Convert to the given unit.

1. 0.72 kiloliters = _____ deciliters

2. 78 qt = _____ gal, _____ qt

3. 52 liters = _____ hectoliters

4. 5 pints = _____ cups

Convert Units of Capacity

Convert to the given unit.

1. 7 gallons = [ ] quarts

conversion factor: $\dfrac{4\ qt}{1\ gal}$

$7\ gal \times \dfrac{4\ qt}{1\ gal}$

$7\ gal = 28\ qt$

2. 5.1 liters = [ ] kiloliters

Move the decimal point **3** places to the left.

5.1 liters = **0.0051** kiloliters

3. 20 qt = [ ] gal

4. 40 L = [ ] mL

5. 16 c = [ ] pt

_____

_____

6. 300 L = [ ] kL

7. 33 pt = [ ] qt [ ] pt

8. 29 cL = [ ] daL

_____

_____

9. 4 pt = [ ] fl oz

10. 7.7 kL = [ ] cL

11. 24 fl oz = [ ] pt [ ] c

_____

_____

Problem Solving REAL WORLD

12. A bottle contains 3.5 liters of water. A second bottle contains 3,750 milliliters of water. How many more milliliters are in the larger bottle than in the smaller bottle?

13. Arnie's car used 100 cups of gasoline during a drive. He paid $3.12 per gallon for gas. How much did the gas cost?

_____

_____

Convert Units of Weight and Mass

In the customary system, weight is the measure of the heaviness of an object. When converting customary units, multiply the initial measurement by a conversion factor.

Convert to the given unit. 19 lb = _____ oz

Step 1 Choose a conversion factor.

16 ounces = 1 pound, so use the conversion factor $\frac{16\ ounces}{1\ pound}$.

Step 2 Multiply by the conversion factor.

$19\ lb \times \frac{16\ oz}{1\ lb} = \frac{19\ \cancel{lb}}{1} \times \frac{16\ oz}{1\ \cancel{lb}} = \frac{304}{1}\ oz = 304\ oz$

So, 19 lb = 304 oz.

Customary Units of Weight
1 pound (lb) = 16 ounces (oz)
1 ton (T) = 2,000 pounds

In the metric system, mass is the measure of the amount of matter in an object. When converting metric units, move the decimal point to multiply or divide by a power of ten.

3.1 dag = _____ mg

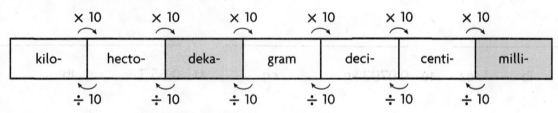

Step 1 Start at the given unit.

Step 2 Move to the unit you are converting to.

Step 3 Move the decimal point that same number of spaces in the same direction. Fill any empty place-value positions with zeros.

So, 3.1 dag = 31,000 mg.

Convert to the given unit.

1. 43.2 dg = _____ hg

2. 4,500 pounds = _____ tons

3. 3.5 grams = _____ milligrams

4. 3 pounds = _____ ounces

Lesson 17
CC.6.RP.3d

Convert Units of Weight and Mass

Convert to the given unit.

1. 5 pounds = [ ] ounces

conversion factor: $\dfrac{16 \text{ oz}}{1 \text{ lb}}$

5 pounds = $5 \cancel{\text{lb}} \times \dfrac{16 \text{ oz}}{1 \cancel{\text{lb}}} = \textbf{80}$ oz

2. 2.36 grams = [ ] hectograms

Move the decimal point **2** places to the left.

2.36 grams = **0.0236** hectogram

3. 48 oz = [ ] lb

4. 30 g = [ ] dg

5. 5 T = [ ] lb

6. 17.2 hg = [ ] g

7. 400 lb = [ ] T

8. 38,600 mg = [ ] dag

9. 87 oz = [ ] lb [ ] oz

10. 0.0793 kg = [ ] cg

11. 0.65 T = [ ] lb

Problem Solving REAL WORLD

12. Maggie bought 52 ounces of swordfish selling for $6.92 per pound. What was the total cost?

13. Three bunches of grapes have masses of 1,000 centigrams, 1,000 decigrams, and 1,000 grams, respectively. What is the total combined mass of the grapes in kilograms?

Transform Units

To solve problems involving different units, use the relationship among units to help you set up a multiplication problem.

Green peppers are on sale for $1.80 per pound. How much would 2.5 pounds of green peppers cost?

Step 1 Identify the units.

You know two quantities: pounds of peppers and total cost per pound. You want to know the cost of 2.5 pounds.

$$\$1.80 \text{ per lb} = \frac{\$1.80}{1 \text{ lb}}$$

Step 2 Determine the relationship among the units.

The answer needs to be in dollars. Set up the multiplication problem so that pounds will divide out.

$$\frac{\$1.80}{1 \text{ lb}} \times 2.5 \text{ lb} = \frac{\$1.80}{1 \text{ lb}} \times \frac{2.5 \text{ lb}}{1} = \$4.50$$

Step 3 Use the relationship.

So, 2.5 pounds of peppers will cost $4.50.

Solve.

1. If 2 bags of cherries cost $5.50, how much do 7 bags cost?

   a. What are you trying to find?

   _____

   b. Set up the problem.

   _____

   c. What is the cost of 7 bags?

2. The area of a living room is 24 square yards. If the width is 12 feet, what is the length of the living room in yards?

   a. What is the width in yards?

   _____

   b. Set up the problem.

   _____

   c. What is the length in yards?

Transform Units

Multiply or divide the quantities.

1. $\frac{62\ g}{1\ day} \times 4\ days$

    $$\frac{62\ g}{1\ day} \times \frac{4\ days}{1} = 248\ g$$

2. 322 sq yd ÷ 23 yd

    $$\frac{322\ sq\ yd}{23\ yd}$$

    $$\frac{322\ yd \times yd}{23\ yd} = 14\ yd$$

3. $\frac{128\ kg}{1\ hr} \times 10\ hr$

4. 136 sq km ÷ 8 km

5. $\frac{88\ lb}{1\ day} \times 12\ days$

_____

6. 154 sq mm ÷ 11 mm

7. $\frac{\$150}{1\ sq\ ft} \times 20\ sq\ ft$

8. 234 sq ft ÷ 18 ft

_____

9. 324 sq yd ÷ 9 yd

10. $\frac{72\ km}{1\ gal} \times 20\ gal$

11. 225 sq dm ÷ 5 dm

_____

Problem Solving  REAL WORLD

12. Green grapes are on sale for $2.50 a pound. How much will 9 pounds cost?

13. A car travels 32 miles for each gallon of gas. How many gallons of gas does it need to travel 192 miles?

_____

Lesson Objective: Solve problems involving distance, rate, and time by applying the strategy *use a formula*.

Problem Solving • Distance, Rate, and Time Formulas

Use a formula to solve the problem.

A bug crawls at a rate of 2 feet per minute. How long will it take the bug to crawl 25 feet?

Read the Problem	Solve the Problem
What do I need to find? I need to find _____ _____.	Write the appropriate formula. $$t = d \div r$$
What information do I need to use? I need to use the _____ the bug crawls and the _____ at which the bug crawls.	Substitute the values for d and r. $$t = \underline{\quad} \text{ ft} \div \frac{2 \text{ ft}}{1 \text{ min}}$$
How will I use the information? First I will choose the formula _____ because I need to find time. Next I will substitute _____ for d and _____ for r. Then I will _____ to find the time.	Rewrite the division as multiplication by the reciprocal. $$t = \frac{25 \text{ ft}}{1} \times \frac{1 \text{ min}}{2 \text{ ft}} = \underline{\quad} \text{ min}$$

1. A family drives for 3 hours at an average rate of 57 miles per hour. How far does the family travel?

2. A train traveled 283.5 miles in 3.5 hours. What was the train's average rate of speed?

Problem Solving • Distance, Rate, and Time Formulas

Read each problem and solve.

1. A downhill skier is traveling at a rate of 0.5 mile per minute. How far will the skier travel in 18 minutes?

$$d = r \times t$$
$$d = \frac{0.5 \text{ mi}}{1 \text{ min}} \times 18 \text{ min}$$
$$d = 9 \text{ miles}$$

2. How long will it take a seal swimming at a speed of 8 miles per hour to travel 52 miles?

_____

3. A dragonfly traveled at a rate of 35 miles per hour for 2.5 hours. What distance did the dragonfly travel?

_____

4. A race car travels 1,212 kilometers in 4 hours. What is the car's rate of speed?

_____

5. A cyclist travels at a rate of 1.8 kilometers per minute. How far will the cyclist travel in 48 minutes?

_____

6. Kim and Jay leave at the same time to travel 25 miles to the beach. Kim drives 9 miles in 12 minutes. Jay drives 10 miles in 15 minutes. If they both continue at the same rate, who will arrive at the beach first?

_____

Lesson 20
COMMON CORE STANDARD CC.6.NS.1

Lesson Objective: Use a model to show
division of fractions.

Model Fraction Division

Use fraction strips to find $\frac{1}{2} \div 3$.

Step 1 $\frac{1}{2} \div 3$ can mean divide $\frac{1}{2}$ into 3 equal parts and
find how much is in each part. Find a fraction strip such
that 3 of that strip make the same length as a single $\frac{1}{2}$-strip.

Step 2 There are three $\frac{1}{6}$-strips in $\frac{1}{2}$, so $\frac{1}{2} \div 3 = \frac{1}{6}$.

Use the model to find the quotient.

1. $\frac{2}{3} \div 6 =$ _____

2. $\frac{1}{4} \div 2 =$ _____

Draw a model with fraction strips. Then find the quotient.

3. $\frac{3}{4} \div 6$

4. $\frac{2}{3} \div 4$

$\frac{3}{4} \div 6 =$ _____

$\frac{2}{3} \div 4 =$ _____

Model Fraction Division

Use the model to find the quotient.

1. $\frac{1}{4} \div 3 = \frac{1}{12}$

2. $\frac{1}{2} \div \frac{2}{12} =$ _____

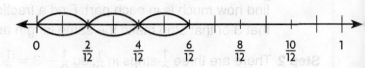

Use fraction strips to find the quotient.

3. $\frac{5}{6} \div \frac{1}{2}$

4. $\frac{2}{3} \div 4$

5. $\frac{1}{2} \div 6$

6. $\frac{1}{3} \div \frac{1}{12}$

_____   _____   _____   _____

Use a number line to find the quotient.

7. How many $\frac{1}{12}$-pint servings of pecans are in $\frac{5}{6}$ pint of pecans?

8. If Jerry runs $\frac{1}{10}$ mile each day, how many days will it take for him to run $\frac{4}{5}$ mile?

_____   _____

Problem Solving REAL WORLD

9. Mrs. Jennings has $\frac{3}{4}$ gallon of paint for an art project. She plans to divide the paint equally into jars. If she puts $\frac{1}{8}$ gallon of paint into each jar, how many jars will she use?

10. If one jar of glue weighs $\frac{1}{12}$ pound, how many jars can Rickie get from $\frac{2}{3}$ pound of glue?

_____   _____

Estimate Quotients

You can use compatible numbers to help you estimate the quotient of fractions and mixed numbers.

Example 1: Estimate $19\frac{5}{7} \div 3\frac{4}{5}$ using compatible numbers.

Step 1 Find whole numbers that are close to $19\frac{5}{7}$ and $3\frac{4}{5}$ that are easy to divide mentally.

  Think: $19\frac{5}{7}$ is close to 20, and $3\frac{4}{5}$ is close to 4.

Step 2 Rewrite the problem and then divide: $20 \div 4 = 5$

So, the estimated quotient is 5.

Example 2: Estimate $6\frac{1}{5} \div \frac{3}{8}$ using compatible numbers.

Step 1 Rewrite the problem using compatible numbers. $6 \div \frac{1}{2}$

Step 2 Divide. Think: How many halves are in 6 wholes? 12

So, the estimated quotient is 12.

Estimate using compatible numbers.

1. $8\frac{1}{6} \div 1\frac{7}{8}$

   a. Rewrite the problem using compatible numbers.

   _____

   b. What is the estimated quotient?

   _____

2. $11\frac{7}{9} \div \frac{4}{10}$

   a. Rewrite the problem using compatible numbers.

   _____

   b. What is the estimated quotient?

   _____

Estimate Quotients

Estimate using compatible numbers.

1. $12\frac{3}{16} \div 3\frac{9}{10}$

   $\downarrow \qquad \downarrow$

   $12 \div 4 = 3$

2. $15\frac{3}{8} \div \frac{1}{2}$

3. $22\frac{1}{5} \div 1\frac{5}{6}$

4. $7\frac{7}{9} \div \frac{4}{7}$

5. $18\frac{1}{4} \div 2\frac{4}{5}$

6. $62\frac{7}{10} \div 8\frac{8}{9}$

7. $\frac{11}{12} \div \frac{1}{5}$

8. $24\frac{3}{4} \div \frac{1}{2}$

9. $\frac{15}{16} \div \frac{1}{7}$

10. $14\frac{7}{8} \div \frac{5}{11}$

11. $53\frac{7}{12} \div 8\frac{11}{12}$

12. $1\frac{1}{6} \div \frac{1}{9}$

Problem Solving REAL WORLD

13. Estimate the number of pieces Sharon will have if she divides $15\frac{1}{3}$ yards of fabric into $4\frac{4}{5}$-yard lengths.

14. Estimate the number of $\frac{1}{2}$-quart containers Ethan can fill from a container with $8\frac{7}{8}$ quarts of water.

Name _____

Divide Fractions

You can multiply by reciprocals to divide fractions.

Write the reciprocal of $\frac{1}{7}$.

To find the reciprocal of a number, switch the numerator and the denominator.

Since $\frac{1}{7} \times \frac{7}{1} = 1$, the reciprocal of $\frac{1}{7}$ is $\frac{7}{1}$.

$\frac{1}{7} \rightarrow \frac{7}{1}$

Find the quotient of $\frac{4}{5} \div \frac{1}{4}$. Write it in simplest form.

Step 1 Find the reciprocal of the second fraction.

Think: $\frac{1}{4} \times \frac{4}{1} = 1$.

The reciprocal of $\frac{1}{4}$ is $\frac{4}{1}$.

Step 2 Write a multiplication problem using the reciprocal of the second fraction.

$\frac{4}{5} \div \frac{1}{4} = \frac{4}{5} \times \frac{4}{1}$

Step 3 Multiply.

$\frac{4}{5} \times \frac{4}{1} = \frac{16}{5}$

Step 4 Simplify.

$\frac{16}{5} = 3\frac{1}{5}$

So, $\frac{4}{5} \div \frac{1}{4} = 3\frac{1}{5}$.

Find the quotient. Write it in simplest form.

1. $\frac{5}{6} \div \frac{2}{3}$

2. $\frac{3}{8} \div \frac{1}{6}$

3. $\frac{2}{3} \div \frac{1}{2}$

4. $6 \div \frac{2}{3}$

5. $12 \div \frac{3}{4}$

6. $\frac{5}{8} \div \frac{1}{2}$

7. $\frac{7}{10} \div \frac{2}{5}$

8. $\frac{5}{6} \div \frac{1}{6}$

The Number System

43

Divide Fractions

Estimate. Then write the quotient in simplest form.

1. $5 \div \frac{1}{6}$

Estimate: 30
$$= 5 \times \frac{6}{1}$$
$$= \frac{30}{1}$$
$$= 30$$

2. $\frac{1}{2} \div \frac{1}{4}$

3. $\frac{4}{5} \div \frac{2}{3}$

4. $\frac{14}{15} \div 7$

5. $\frac{2}{5} \div \frac{7}{10}$

6. $\frac{5}{9} \div \frac{5}{7}$

7. $4 \div \frac{4}{5}$

8. $1 \div \frac{3}{4}$

9. $8 \div \frac{1}{3}$

10. $\frac{12}{21} \div \frac{2}{3}$

11. $\frac{5}{6} \div \frac{5}{12}$

12. $\frac{5}{8} \div \frac{1}{2}$

13. Joy ate $\frac{1}{4}$ of a pizza. If she divides the rest of the pizza into pieces equal to $\frac{1}{8}$ pizza for her family, how many pieces will her family get?

14. Hideko has $\frac{3}{5}$ yard of ribbon to tie on balloons for the festival. Each balloon will need $\frac{3}{10}$ yard of ribbon. How many balloons can Hideko tie with ribbon?

Problem Solving  REAL WORLD

15. Rick knows that 1 cup of glue weighs $\frac{1}{18}$ pound. He has $\frac{2}{3}$ pound of glue. How many cups of glue does he have?

16. Mrs. Jennings had $\frac{5}{7}$ gallon of paint. She gave $\frac{1}{7}$ gallon each to some students. How many students received paint if Mrs. Jennings gave away all the paint?

Model Mixed Number Division

Use pattern blocks to find the quotient of $3\frac{1}{2} \div \frac{1}{6}$.

Step 1 Model 3 with 3 hexagon blocks.

Model $\frac{1}{2}$ with 1 trapezoid block.

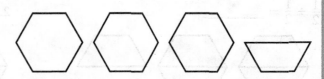

Step 2 Find a block that shows $\frac{1}{6}$.

6 triangle blocks are equal to 1 hexagon.

So, a triangle block shows $\frac{1}{6}$.

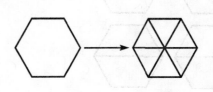

Step 3 Cover your model with triangle blocks.

Count the triangles.
There are 21 triangle blocks.

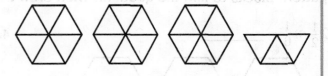

So, $3\frac{1}{2} \div \frac{1}{6} = 21$.

Use the model to find the quotient.

1. $2\frac{1}{3} \div \frac{1}{6} =$ _____

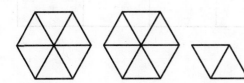

2. $2\frac{1}{2} \div \frac{1}{2} =$ _____

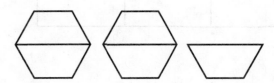

Use pattern blocks to find the quotient. Then draw the model.

3. $1\frac{1}{2} \div \frac{1}{6} =$ _____

4. $1\frac{2}{3} \div \frac{1}{3} =$ _____

The Number System

Model Mixed Number Division

Use the model to find the quotient.

1. $4\frac{1}{2} \div \frac{1}{2} =$ ___**9**___

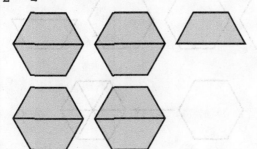

2. $3\frac{1}{3} \div \frac{1}{6} =$ _____

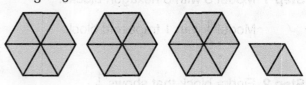

Use pattern blocks to find the quotient. Then draw the model.

3. $2\frac{1}{2} \div \frac{1}{6} =$ _____

4. $1\frac{1}{2} \div \frac{1}{2} =$ _____

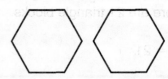

Draw a model to solve.

5. $2\frac{3}{4} \div 2 =$ _____

6. $3\frac{1}{3} \div 3 =$ _____

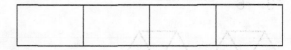

Problem Solving

7. Marty has $2\frac{4}{5}$ quarts of juice. He pours the same amount of juice into 2 bottles. How much does he pour into each bottle?

8. How many $\frac{1}{3}$-pound servings are in $4\frac{2}{3}$ pounds of cheese?

_____   _____

Divide Mixed Numbers

To divide mixed numbers, first rewrite the mixed numbers as fractions greater than 1. Then multiply the dividend by the reciprocal of the divisor.

Find the quotient of $7\frac{1}{2} \div 2\frac{1}{2}$. Write it in simplest form.

Step 1 Write the mixed numbers as fractions.

$$7\frac{1}{2} \div 2\frac{1}{2} = \frac{15}{2} \div \frac{5}{2}$$

Step 2 Use the reciprocal of the divisor to write a multiplication problem.

$$= \frac{15}{2} \times \frac{2}{5}$$

Step 3 Simplify. Look for common factors in the numerators and denominators. Divide out the common factors.

$$= \frac{\overset{3}{\cancel{15}}}{\underset{1}{\cancel{2}}} \times \frac{\overset{1}{\cancel{2}}}{\underset{1}{\cancel{5}}}$$

Step 4 Multiply and simplify the product.

$$= \frac{3}{1} = 3$$

So, $7\frac{1}{2} \div 2\frac{1}{2} = 3$.

Find the quotient. Write it in simplest form.

1. $\frac{3}{4} \div 1\frac{1}{2}$

2. $4\frac{1}{2} \div 1\frac{3}{4}$

3. $8 \div 2\frac{3}{4}$

4. $5\frac{5}{8} \div 1\frac{1}{2}$

5. $2\frac{5}{8} \div \frac{5}{6}$

6. $\frac{4}{7} \div 1\frac{2}{3}$

7. $4\frac{7}{10} \div \frac{4}{5}$

8. $4\frac{2}{5} \div \frac{8}{15}$

9. $24 \div 2\frac{2}{3}$

10. $8\frac{3}{4} \div 2\frac{1}{3}$

11. $3\frac{7}{8} \div 4$

12. $2\frac{5}{8} \div 3\frac{1}{2}$

Name _____

Divide Mixed Numbers

Estimate. Then write the quotient in simplest form.

1. $2\frac{1}{2} \div 2\frac{1}{3}$

Estimate: $2 \div 2 = 1$

$2\frac{1}{2} \div 2\frac{1}{3} = \frac{5}{2} \div \frac{7}{3}$

$= \frac{5}{2} \times \frac{3}{7}$

$= \frac{15}{14}$ or $1\frac{1}{14}$

2. $2\frac{2}{3} \div 1\frac{1}{3}$

3. $2 \div 3\frac{5}{8}$

4. $1\frac{13}{15} \div 1\frac{2}{5}$

5. $10 \div 6\frac{2}{3}$

6. $2\frac{3}{5} \div 1\frac{1}{25}$

7. $2\frac{1}{5} \div 2$

8. Sid and Jill hiked $4\frac{1}{8}$ miles in the morning and $1\frac{7}{8}$ miles in the afternoon. How many times as far did they hike in the morning as in the afternoon?

9. Kim has $2\frac{1}{2}$ cups of peaches. How many $\frac{1}{4}$-cup servings can she make?

Problem Solving REAL WORLD

10. It takes Nim $2\frac{2}{3}$ hours to weave a basket. He worked Monday through Friday, 8 hours a day. How many baskets did he make?

11. A tree grows $1\frac{3}{4}$ feet per year. How long will it take the tree to grow from a height of $21\frac{1}{4}$ feet to a height of 37 feet?

Problem Solving • Fraction Operations

Draw a model to solve the problem.

Naomi cuts a $\frac{3}{4}$-foot paper roll into sections, each $\frac{1}{16}$ foot long. If she discards $\frac{1}{8}$ foot of the roll, how many sections does she still have?

Read the Problem	Solve the Problem
What do I need to find? The number _____ _____ .	Draw a model to solve the problem. Show $\frac{3}{4}$. Divide $\frac{3}{4}$ into eighths.
What information do I need to use? Naomi starts with _____ _____ . Each section is _____ . She discards _____ .	She discarded $\frac{1}{8}$, so cross out 1 eighth. $\frac{3}{4} - \frac{1}{8} = \frac{5}{8}$
How will I use the information? I will _____ to find _____ _____ .	Divide $\frac{5}{8}$ into sixteenths. There are 10 sixteenths in $\frac{5}{8}$, so she has 10 sections left.

1. Jeff has $\frac{2}{3}$ gallon of sherbet. He gives each of his friends one $\frac{1}{12}$-gallon scoop. There is $\frac{1}{6}$ gallon left in the carton. How many friends got sherbet?

2. A branch measuring $8\frac{7}{8}$ feet was cut from a tree. Crystal made $2\frac{3}{16}$ feet walking sticks from the branch. She discarded $\frac{1}{8}$ foot of the branch. How many walking sticks did she make from the branch?

Problem Solving • Fraction Operations

Read each problem and solve.

1. $\frac{2}{3}$ of a pizza was left over. A group of friends divided the leftover pizza into pieces each equal to $\frac{1}{18}$ of the original pizza. After each friend took one piece, $\frac{1}{6}$ of the leftover pizza remained. How many friends were in the group?

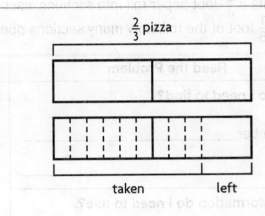

$\frac{2}{3}$ pizza

taken   left

_____ 9

2. Sarah's craft project uses pieces of yarn that are $\frac{1}{8}$ yard long. She has a piece of yarn that is 3 yards long. How many $\frac{1}{8}$-yard pieces can she cut and still have $1\frac{1}{4}$ yards left?

_____

3. Alex opens a 1-pint container of orange butter. He spreads $\frac{1}{16}$ of the butter on his bread. Then he divides the rest of the butter into $\frac{3}{4}$-pint containers. How many $\frac{3}{4}$-pint containers is he able to fill?

_____

4. Kaitlin buys $\frac{9}{10}$ pound of orange slices. She eats $\frac{1}{3}$ of them and divides the rest equally into 3 bags. How much is in each bag?

_____

Divide Multi-Digit Numbers

When you divide multi-digit whole numbers, you can estimate to check if the quotient is reasonable.

Divide 399 ÷ 42.

Step 1 Estimate, using compatible numbers.

400 and 40 are compatible numbers because 40 divides evenly into 400.

$400 \div 40 = 10$

Step 2 Divide the original numbers.

$$\begin{array}{r} 9\ \text{r}21 \\ 42\overline{)399} \\ -378 \\ \hline 21 \end{array}$$

Step 3 You can write the remainder as a fraction. Use the remainder for the numerator, and the divisor for the denominator. Simplify if possible.

$$\frac{21 \div 21}{42 \div 21} = \frac{1}{2}$$

$$399 \div 42 = 9\frac{1}{2}$$

Step 4 Compare the quotient with your estimate.

Since $9\frac{1}{2}$ is close to 10, the quotient is reasonable.

Estimate. Then find the quotient. Write the remainder, if any, with an r.

1. $17\overline{)965}$

2. $29\overline{)4,380}$

3. $62\overline{)1,178}$

_____ _____ _____

Estimate. Then find the quotient. Write the remainder, if any, as a fraction.

4. $836 \div 32$

5. $1,392 \div 18$

6. $2,518 \div 48$

_____ _____ _____

Divide Multi-Digit Numbers

Estimate. Then find the quotient. Write the remainder, if any, with an r.

1.
```
        13
  55)715
     55
    165
    165
      0
```
Estimate:
700 ÷ 50 = 15

2. 19)800

3. 68)1,025

_____

Estimate. Then find the quotient. Write the remainder, if any, as a fraction.

4. 32)1,504

5. 20)1,683

6. 35)955

_____

_____

7. 1,034 ÷ 22

8. 14,124 ÷ 44

9. 11,629 ÷ 29

_____

_____

Find the least whole number that can replace ▮ to make the statement true.

10. ▮ ÷ 7 > 800

11. ▮ ÷ 21 > 13

12. 15 < ▮ ÷ 400

_____

_____

Problem Solving REAL WORLD

13. A plane flew a total of 2,220 miles. Its average speed was 555 miles per hour. How many hours did the plane fly?

14. A van is carrying 486 pounds. There are 27 boxes in the van. What is the average weight of each box in the van?

_____

_____

Add and Subtract Decimals

Estimate 84.9 + 0.463. Then find the sum.

84.9 → 85
+ 0.463 → + 0
——————
85

Round each number to the nearest whole number.
So, a good estimate is 85.

Now line up the decimal points. Then add.

Write zeros as placeholders.

84.9	→	84.900	Regroup. →	84.900 (1)
+ 0.463	→	+ 0.463	→	+ 0.463
				85.363

The answer is close to the estimate. So, the answer is reasonable.

Evaluate 45.2 − (27.93 − 10.84) using the order of operations.

Perform the operations in parentheses.

27.93
− 10.84
————
17.09

Subtract.

45.20
− 17.09
————
28.11

So, 45.2 − (27.93 − 10.84) is 28.11.

Estimate. Then find the sum or difference.

1. 62.38
   + 26.92

2. 48.28
   − 9.41

3. 81.04
   52
   + 16.44

4. 27.29
   − 19.39

_____

5. 743.5 − 462.87

6. 98.01 + 52.003

7. 74.9 − 16.227

_____

Evaluate using the order of operations.

8. (235.152 + 77.12) − 46.326

9. 11.024 − (1.518 + 1.7)

_____

The Number System

Add and Subtract Decimals

Estimate. Then find the sum or difference.

1. 43.53 + 27.67

$$40 + 30 = 70$$

$$\begin{array}{r} 43.53 \\ + 27.67 \\ \hline 71.20 \end{array}$$

2. 17 + 3.6 + 4.049

3. 3.49 − 2.75

4. 5.07 − 2.148

5. 3.92 + 16 + 0.085

6. 41.98 + 13.5 + 27.338

Evaluate using the order of operations.

7. 8.4 + (13.1 − 0.6)

8. 34.7 − (12.07 + 4.9)

9. (24.3 − 1.12) + 5.18

10. (32.45 − 4.8) − 2.06

Problem Solving  REAL WORLD

11. The average annual rainfall in Clearview is 38 inches. This year, 29.777 inches fell. How much less rain fell this year than falls in an average year?

12. At the theater, the Worth family spent $18.00 on adult tickets, $16.50 on children's tickets, and $11.75 on refreshments. How much did they spend in all?

Name _____

Lesson 28
COMMON CORE STANDARD CC.6.NS.3
Lesson Objective: Fluently multiply multi-digit decimals.

Multiply Decimals

When multiplying decimals, you can estimate to help you place the decimal point in the product.

Estimate $32.05 × 7.4. Then find the product.

Step 1 Estimate. Round each factor to the nearest ten or the nearest whole number.

$32.05 is about $30, and 7.4 is close to 7.

So, the product should be close to $210.

```
 32.05          30
× 7.4   ⟶     × 7
               210
```

Step 2 Multiply.

```
  32.05
×   7.4
 12820
224350
237170
```

Step 3 Place the decimal point. Remember, the product is estimated to be 210. Place the decimal point so that the product is close in value to 210.

237.17

So, the product is $237.17.

Estimate. Then find the product.

1. 8.6
     × 4.1

2. 12.8 × 2.21

3. $8.65 × 9.2

Evaluate using the order of operations.

4. 19.5 × (21.04 − 18.7)

5. 11.7 + (7.92 × 8.5)

Multiply Decimals

Estimate. Then find the product.

1. 5.69×7.8

$6 \times 8 = 48$

$$\begin{array}{r} 5.69 \\ \times\ 7.8 \\ \hline 4552 \\ 39830 \\ \hline 44.382 \end{array}$$

2. 4.8×1.7

3. 3.92×0.051

4. 2.365×12.4

5. 305.08×1.5

6. 61.8×1.7

7. 35.80×5.6

8. 1.9×8.43

Evaluate the expression using the order of operations.

9. $(13.1 \times 3) + 5.21$

10. $4 \times (15 - 4.55)$

11. $20.5 - (2 \times 8.1)$

Problem Solving REAL WORLD

12. Blaine exchanges $100 for yen before going to Japan. If each U.S. dollar is worth 88.353 yen, how many yen should Blaine receive?

13. A camera costs 115 Canadian dollars. If each Canadian dollar is worth 0.952 U.S. dollars, how much will the camera cost in U.S. dollars?

Divide Decimals by Whole Numbers

When you divide a decimal by a whole number, place the decimal point in the quotient directly above the decimal point in the dividend.

Estimate 12)60.84. **Then find the quotient.**

Step 1 Estimate the quotient, using compatible numbers.

60 and 12 are compatible numbers because
12 divides evenly into 60.

$60 \div 12 = 5$

Step 2 Use long division to divide.

```
      5.07
 12)60.84
   -60 ↓
       8
      -0 ↓
      84
     -84
       0
```

Place the decimal point in the quotient directly above the decimal point in the dividend.

Since 8 tenths cannot be shared among 12 groups, write 0 as a placeholder in the tenths place.

So, $60.84 \div 12 = 5.07$.

Estimate. Then find the quotient.

1. $16.48 \div 8$ **2.** $191.7 \div 9$ **3.** 4)21.64   **4.** 14)41.44   **5.** 21)49.14

_____ _____ _____ _____ _____

6. 6)3.78   **7.** $92.8 \div 16$ **8.** 5)1.725   **9.** 11)135.3   **10.** 9)7.29

_____ _____ _____ _____ _____

Name _____

Divide Decimals by Whole Numbers

Estimate. Then find the quotient.

1. $1.284 \div 12$

$$1.2 \div 12 = 0.1$$

```
      0.107
12)1.284
   -12
      8
    - 0
     84
    -84
      0
```

2. $24.012 \div 6$

3. $9)\overline{2.43}$

4. $4)\overline{1.52}$

5. $6.51 \div 3$

6. $25.65 \div 15$

7. $12)\overline{2.436}$

8. $11)\overline{46.2}$

Evaluate using the order of operations.

9. $(8 - 2.96) \div 3$

10. $(7.772 - 2.38) \div 8$

11. $(53.2 + 35.7) \div 7$

Problem Solving REAL WORLD

12. Jake earned $10.44 interest on his savings account for an 18-month period. What was the average amount of interest Jake earned on his savings account per month?

13. Gloria worked for 6 hours a day for 2 days at the bank and earned $114.24. How much did she earn per hour?

Name _____

Lesson 30

COMMON CORE STANDARD CC.6.NS.3

Lesson Objective: Fluently divide whole numbers and decimals by decimals.

Divide with Decimals

When dividing a decimal by a decimal, rewrite the divisor as a whole number. To keep an equivalent problem, move the decimal point in the dividend the same direction and number of places.

Rewrite the problem so that the divisor is a whole number.

300.7 ÷ 1.24

300.7 is the dividend and 1.24 is the divisor.

Change the Divisor

1.24 × 100 = 124

Multiply 1.24 by 100 because 1.24 has two decimal places.

Change the Dividend

300.7 × 100 = 30,070

To keep an equivalent problem, multiply the dividend by the same number, 100.

So, 300.7 ÷ 1.24 is the same problem as 30,070 ÷ 124.

Find the quotient.

0.55)‾24.2‾

Step 1

Rewrite the problem so that the divisor is a whole number.

Divisor	**Dividend**
0.55 × 100 = 55	24.2 × 100 = 2,420

Step 2

Divide.

```
      44
55)2420
  -220
   220
  -220
     0
```

So, 24.2 ÷ 0.55 = 44.

Rewrite the problem so that the divisor is a whole number.

1. 8.9 ÷ 0.62   **2.** 21.05 ÷ 0.2   **3.** 512.3 ÷ 2.71   **4.** 18.62 ÷ 0.02

Find the quotient.

5. 8.75 ÷ 0.7   **6.** 72.24 ÷ 5.6   **7.** 0.21)‾1.3545‾   **8.** 2.17)‾18.228‾

The Number System

Divide with Decimals

Estimate. Then find the quotient.

1. 43.18 ÷ 3.4   **2.** 4.185 ÷ 0.93   **3.** 6.3)‾25.83   **4.** 0.8)‾1.008

$$\underline{44 \div 4 = 11}$$

$$\begin{array}{r} 12.7 \\ 34)\overline{431.8} \\ -34 \\ \hline 91 \\ -68 \\ \hline 238 \\ -238 \\ \hline 0 \end{array}$$

Find the quotient.

5. 9.12 ÷ 0.4   **6.** 0.143 ÷ 0.55   **7.** 0.6)‾3.558   **8.** 0.24)‾1.8

_____   _____   _____   _____

Evaluate using the order of operations.

9. 4.92 ÷ (0.8 − 0.12 ÷ 0.3)   **10.** 0.86 ÷ 5 − 0.3 × 0.5   **11.** 17.28 ÷ (1.32 − 0.24) × 0.6

_____   _____   _____

Problem Solving  REAL WORLD

12. If Amanda walks at an average speed of 2.72 miles per hour, how long will it take her to walk 6.8 miles?

_____

13. Chad cycled 62.3 miles in 3.5 hours. If he cycled at a constant speed, how far did he cycle in 1 hour?

_____

© Houghton Mifflin Harcourt Publishing Company

Lesson 31

COMMON CORE STANDARD CC.6.NS.4
Lesson Objective: Write the prime
factorization of numbers.

Prime Factorization

A number written as the product of prime numbers is called the **prime
factorization** of that number. To break a number down into its prime
factors, divide it by prime numbers. The first eight prime numbers are
listed below.

2, 3, 5, 7, 11, 13, 17, 19

**You can use a factor tree to find the prime
factorization of a number.**

Divide the number by the least
prime factor possible. Try 2, 3,
5, and so on.

Break 55 down because it is
not a prime number.

The numbers at the bottom of
the branches are all prime.

**You can use a ladder diagram to find the
prime factorization of a number.**

```
⑤ | 165
③ | 33
⑪ | 11
     | 1
```

165 ends in 5, so it is divisible
by 5. Divide 165 by 5.

Write the quotient below 165.

The sum of the digits in
33 is divisible by 3, so divide
33 by 3.

11 is prime. Divide 11 by itself.

The bottom number is 1 and
all the numbers to the left are
prime.

**Write the number as a product of prime factors. The factors should be
in order from least to greatest.**

So, the prime factorization of 165 is 3 × 5 × 11.

Find the prime factorization of the number.

1. 21

2. 130

3. 84

_____   _____   _____

Prime Factorization

Find the prime factorization.

1. 44

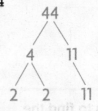

$2 \times 2 \times 11$

2. 90

3. 48

4. 204

5. 400

6. 112

Write the number whose prime factorization is given.

7. $3 \times 3 \times 11$

8. $2 \times 2 \times 7 \times 13$

9. $2 \times 3 \times 3 \times 3$

Problem Solving REAL WORLD

10. A computer code is based on the prime factorization of 160. Find the prime factorization of 160.

11. The combination for a lock is a 3-digit number. The digits are the prime factors of 42 listed from least to greatest. What is the combination for the lock?

Least Common Multiple

The **least common multiple**, or **LCM**, is the least number that two or more numbers have in common in their list of nonzero multiples.

Find the LCM of 3 and 9.

List the first ten nonzero multiples of each number:

    Multiples of 3: 3, 6, 9, 12, 15, 18, 21, 24, 27, 30

    Multiples of 9: 9, 18, 27, 36, 45, 54, 63, 72, 81, 90

The first three nonzero multiples that 3 and 9 have in common are 9, 18, and 27.

So, the LCM of 3 and 9 is 9.

Find the LCM.

1. 4, 10
List the first ten multiples for each number.

Multiples of 4: 4, 8, _____, 16, _____, 24,

_____, _____, 36, _____

Multiples of 10: 10, _____, 30, _____, 50,

_____, 70, _____, _____, 100

List the numbers that appear in both lists.

Common multiples: _____ and _____

The LCM of 4 and 10 is _____.

2. 6, 8
List the first ten multiples for each number.

Multiples of 6: _____

_____

Multiples of 8: _____

_____

List the numbers that appear in both lists.

Common multiples: _____

The LCM of 6 and 8 is _____.

3. 5, 20

4. 6, 15

5. 12, 30

_____

6. 7, 14

7. 10, 15

8. 6, 18

_____   _____   _____

Least Common Multiple

Find the LCM.

1. 2, 7

Multiples of 2: 2, 4, 6, 8, 10, 12, 14
Multiples of 7: 7, 14

LCM: __**14**__

2. 4, 12

LCM: _____

3. 10, 4

LCM: _____

4. 6, 9

LCM: _____

5. 5, 4

LCM: _____

6. 8, 10

LCM: _____

7. 8, 20

LCM: _____

8. 5, 8, 4

LCM: _____

9. 12, 8, 24

LCM: _____

Write the unknown number for the ▪.

10. 3, ▪   LCM: 21

11. ▪, 7   LCM: 63

12. 10, 5   LCM: ▪

▪ = _____

▪ = _____

▪ = _____

Problem Solving 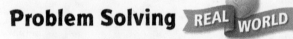 REAL WORLD

13. Juanita is making necklaces to give as presents. She plans to put 15 beads on each necklace. Beads are sold in packages of 20. What is the least number of packages she can buy to make necklaces and have no beads left over?

_____

14. Pencils are sold in packages of 10, and erasers are sold in packages of 6. What is the least number of pencils and erasers you can buy so that there is one pencil for each eraser with none left over?

_____

Name _____

Lesson 33
COMMON CORE STANDARD CC.6.NS.4

Lesson Objective: Find the greatest common factor of two whole numbers.

Greatest Common Factor

A **common factor** is a number that is a factor of two or more numbers.
The **greatest common factor**, or **GCF**, is the greatest factor that two
or more numbers have in common.

Find the common factors of 9 and 27. Then find the GCF.

Step 1
List the factors of each number.
Factors of 9: 1, 3, 9
Factors of 27: 1, 3, 9, 27

Step 2
Identify the common factors.
Common factors of 9 and 27:
1, 3, 9

The greatest of the common factors is 9.
So, the GCF of 9 and 27 is 9.

You can use the GCF and the Distributive Property to express the sum
of two numbers as a product.

Write 9 + 27 as a product.

Step 1
Write each number as the product of
the GCF and another factor.

Step 2
Write an expression multiplying the GCF
and the sum of the two factors from Step 1.

$9 = 9 \times 1 \qquad 27 = 9 \times 3$ $9 \times (1 + 3)$

The product $9 \times (1 + 3)$ has the same value as $9 + 27$.

So, $9 + 27 = 9 \times (1 + 3)$.

Find the GCF.

1. 18, 45

2. 33, 66

3. 72, 96

4. 50, 80

Use the GCF and the Distributive Property to express the sum as a product.

5. 18 + 24

6. 15 + 75

7. 36 + 54

8. 16 + 20

_____   _____   _____   _____

Greatest Common Factor

List the common factors. Circle the greatest common factor.

1. 25 and 10

2. 36 and 90

3. 45 and 60

_____ 1, ⑤ _____

Find the GCF.

4. 2, 8

5. 6, 15

6. 14, 18

_____

7. 6, 48

8. 20, 50

9. 16, 100

_____

Use the GCF and the Distributive Property to express the sum as a product.

10. 20 + 35

11. 18 + 27

12. 64 + 40

_____

Problem Solving REAL WORLD

13. Jerome is making prizes for a game at the school fair. He has two bags of different candies, one with 15 pieces of candy and one with 20 pieces. Every prize will have one kind of candy, the same number of pieces, and the greatest number of pieces possible. How many candies should be in each prize?

14. There are 24 sixth graders and 40 seventh graders. Mr. Chan wants to divide both grades into groups of equal size, with the greatest possible number of students in each group. How many students should be in each group?

_____

Problem Solving • Apply the Greatest Common Factor

Use the Distributive Property and a diagram to solve.

Bethany is packing cookies for her drama club's bake sale. She has 28 oatmeal cookies and 36 peanut butter cookies to pack. Each bag will contain only one kind of cookie, and every bag will have the same number of cookies. What is the greatest number of cookies she can pack in each bag? How many bags of each kind will there be?

Read the Problem	Solve the Problem
What do I need to find? I need to find the _____ number of cookies for each _____ and the number of bags for _____.	**Step 1** Find the GCF of 28 and 36. Use prime factorization. $28 = 2 \times 2 \times 7 \qquad 36 = 2 \times 2 \times 3 \times 3$ Multiply common prime factors: $2 \times 2 =$ ____ GCF: ____
What information do I need to use? I need to use the number of _____ _____ and the number of _____ _____	**Step 2** Write 28 as a product of the GCF and another factor. $\qquad 28 = 4 \times$ ____ Write 36 as a product of the GCF and another factor. $\qquad 36 = 4 \times$ ____
How will I use the information? First, I can find the _____ _____. Then I can draw a diagram showing the _____.	**Step 3** Use the Distributive Property to write $28 + 36$ as a product. $\qquad 28 + 36 =$ _____ $4 \times ($ ____ $+$ ____ $)$ **Step 4** Use the product to draw a diagram of the bags of cookies. Write O for each oatmeal cookie and P for each peanut butter cookie.

So, each bag will have ____ cookies. There will be ____ bags of

oatmeal cookies and ____ bags of peanut butter cookies.

1. Jacob is putting 18 nonfiction and 30 fiction books on bookshelves. Each shelf will have only fiction or only nonfiction, and every shelf will have the same number of books. What is the greatest number of books for each shelf, and how many shelves will there be for each type of book?

The Number System

Problem Solving • Apply the Greatest Common Factor

Read the problem and solve.

1. Ashley is bagging 32 pumpkin muffins and 28 banana muffins for some friends. Each bag will hold only one type of muffin. Each bag will hold the same number of muffins. What is the greatest number of muffins she can put in each bag? How many bags of each type of muffin will there be?

   GCF: 4

   $32 = 4 \times 8$

   $28 = 4 \times 7$

   $32 + 28 = 4 \times (8 + 7)$

   So, there will be __8__ bags of pumpkin muffins and __7__ bags of banana muffins,

   with __4__ muffins in each bag.

2. Patricia is separating 16 soccer cards and 22 baseball cards into groups. Each group will have the same number of cards, and each group will have only one kind of sports card. What is the greatest number of cards she can put in each group? How many groups of each type will there be?

   _____

3. Bryan is setting chairs in rows for a graduation ceremony. He has 50 black chairs and 60 white chairs. Each row will have the same number of chairs, and each row will have the same color chair. What is the greatest number of chairs that he can fit in each row? How many rows of each color chair will there be?

   _____

4. A store clerk is bagging spices. He has 18 teaspoons of cinnamon and 30 teaspoons of nutmeg. Each bag needs to contain the same number of teaspoons, and each bag can contain only one spice. How many teaspoons of spice should the clerk put in each bag? How many bags of each spice will there be?

   _____

5. A teacher is placing counters in bags for students. There are 24 blue counters and 56 yellow counters. Each bag needs to have the same number of counters, and each bag can only contain one color. How many counters should the teacher place in each bag, and how many bags of each color will there be?

   _____

Multiply Fractions

To multiply fractions, you can multiply numerators and multiply denominators. Write the product in simplest form.

Find $\dfrac{3}{10} \times \dfrac{4}{5}$.

Step 1 Multiply numerators. Multiply denominators.

$$\dfrac{3}{10} \times \dfrac{4}{5} = \dfrac{3 \times 4}{10 \times 5} = \dfrac{12}{50}$$

Step 2 Write the product in simplest form.

$$\dfrac{12}{50} = \dfrac{12 \div 2}{50 \div 2} = \dfrac{6}{25}$$

So, $\dfrac{3}{10} \times \dfrac{4}{5} = \dfrac{6}{25}$.

To simplify an expression with fractions, follow the order of operations as you would with whole numbers.

Find $\left(\dfrac{5}{7} - \dfrac{3}{14}\right) \times \dfrac{1}{10}$.

Step 1 Perform the operation in parentheses. To subtract, write an equivalent fraction using a common denominator.

Multiply the numerator and denominator of $\dfrac{5}{7}$ by 2 to get a common denominator of 14.

$$\left(\dfrac{5}{7} - \dfrac{3}{14}\right) \times \dfrac{1}{10} = \left(\dfrac{5 \times 2}{7 \times 2} - \dfrac{3}{14}\right) \times \dfrac{1}{10}$$

$$= \left(\dfrac{10}{14} - \dfrac{3}{14}\right) \times \dfrac{1}{10}$$

$$= \dfrac{7}{14} \times \dfrac{1}{10}$$

Step 2 Multiply numerators. Multiply denominators.

$$= \dfrac{7 \times 1}{14 \times 10} = \dfrac{7}{140}$$

Step 3 Write the product in simplest form. Divide the numerator and the denominator by the GCF.

$$= \dfrac{7 \div 7}{140 \div 7} = \dfrac{1}{20}$$

So, $\left(\dfrac{5}{7} - \dfrac{3}{14}\right) \times \dfrac{1}{10} = \dfrac{1}{20}$.

Find the product. Write the product in simplest form.

1. $\dfrac{3}{4} \times \dfrac{1}{5}$

2. $\dfrac{4}{7} \times \dfrac{5}{12}$

3. $\dfrac{3}{8} \times \dfrac{2}{9}$

4. $\dfrac{4}{5} \times \dfrac{5}{8}$

_____ _____ _____ _____

Evaluate using the order of operations.

5. $\dfrac{7}{8} - \dfrac{5}{6} \times \dfrac{1}{2}$

6. $\left(\dfrac{4}{5} + \dfrac{1}{3}\right) \times \dfrac{5}{9}$

7. $\dfrac{3}{4} \times \dfrac{2}{5} + \dfrac{1}{4}$

8. $\dfrac{3}{10} \times \left(\dfrac{2}{3} - \dfrac{1}{6}\right)$

_____ _____ _____ _____

Multiply Fractions

Find the product. Write it in simplest form.

1. $\frac{4}{5} \times \frac{7}{8} = \dfrac{28}{40}$

   $= \dfrac{7}{10}$

2. $3 \times \frac{1}{6}$

3. $\frac{5}{9} \times \frac{3}{4}$

4. $\frac{4}{7} \times \frac{1}{2}$

5. $\frac{1}{8} \times 20$

6. $\frac{4}{5} \times \frac{3}{8}$

7. $\frac{6}{7} \times \frac{7}{9}$

8. $1\frac{1}{8} \times \frac{1}{9}$

9. $\frac{1}{14} \times 28$

10. $\frac{3}{4} \times \frac{1}{3} \times \frac{2}{5}$

11. Karen raked $\frac{3}{5}$ of the yard. Minni raked $\frac{1}{3}$ of the amount Karen raked. How much of the yard did Minni rake?

12. $\frac{3}{8}$ of the pets in the pet show are dogs. $\frac{2}{3}$ of the dogs have long hair. What fraction of the pets are dogs with long hair?

Evaluate using the order of operations.

13. $\left(\frac{1}{2} + \frac{3}{8}\right) \times 8$

14. $\frac{3}{4} \times \left(1 - \frac{1}{9}\right)$

15. $4 \times \frac{1}{8} \times \frac{3}{10}$

16. $6 \times \left(\frac{4}{5} + \frac{2}{10}\right) \times \frac{2}{3}$

Problem Solving REAL WORLD

17. Jason ran $\frac{5}{7}$ of the distance around the school track. Sara ran $\frac{4}{5}$ of Jason's distance. What fraction of the total distance around the track did Sara run?

18. A group of students attend a math club. Half of the students are boys and $\frac{4}{9}$ of the boys have brown eyes. What fraction of the group are boys with brown eyes?

Lesson 36

COMMON CORE STANDARD CC.6.NS.4

Lesson Objective: Simplify fractional factors by using the greatest common factor.

Simplify Factors

Sometimes you can simplify before you multiply fractions.

Find the product of $\frac{5}{6} \times \frac{4}{15}$. Simplify before multiplying.

Step 1 Rewrite as a single fraction.

$$\frac{5 \times 4}{6 \times 15}$$

Step 2 Look for numbers in the numerator that have common factors with numbers in the denominator. Find the GCF.

The GCF of 5 and 15 is 5.
The GCF of 6 and 4 is 2.

$$\frac{\boxed{5} \times \boxed{4}}{\boxed{6} \times \boxed{15}}$$

Step 3 Divide.

$$5 \div 5 = 1 \qquad\qquad 6 \div 2 = 3$$
$$15 \div 5 = 3 \qquad\qquad 4 \div 2 = 2$$

$$\frac{\overset{1}{\cancel{5}} \times \overset{2}{\cancel{4}}}{\underset{3}{\cancel{6}} \times \underset{3}{\cancel{15}}}$$

Step 4 Rewrite the fraction with the new numbers. Multiply the numerators. Multiply the denominators.

$$\frac{1 \times 2}{3 \times 3} = \frac{2}{9}$$

So, $\frac{5}{6} \times \frac{4}{15} = \frac{2}{9}$.

Find the product. Simplify before multiplying.

1. $\frac{4}{9} \times \frac{3}{14}$

2. $\frac{3}{4} \times \frac{2}{5}$

3. $\frac{3}{20} \times \frac{5}{6}$

_____   _____   _____

4. $\frac{7}{10} \times \frac{4}{5}$

5. $\frac{3}{16} \times \frac{8}{27}$

6. $\frac{1}{8} \times \frac{2}{7}$

_____   _____   _____

Simplify Factors

Find the product. Simplify before multiplying.

1. $\dfrac{8}{9} \times \dfrac{5}{12} = \dfrac{^2 8 \times 5}{9 \times 12_3}$

    $= \dfrac{10}{27}$

2. $\dfrac{3}{4} \times \dfrac{16}{21}$

    _____

3. $\dfrac{15}{20} \times \dfrac{2}{5}$

    _____

4. $\dfrac{9}{18} \times \dfrac{2}{3}$

5. $\dfrac{9}{10} \times \dfrac{5}{27}$

    _____

6. $\dfrac{3}{4} \times \dfrac{7}{30}$

    _____

7. $\dfrac{25}{26} \times \dfrac{1}{5}$

    _____

8. $\dfrac{8}{15} \times \dfrac{15}{32}$

9. $\dfrac{12}{21} \times \dfrac{7}{9}$

    _____

10. $\dfrac{1}{15} \times \dfrac{5}{8}$

    _____

11. $\dfrac{18}{22} \times \dfrac{8}{9}$

    _____

12. $\dfrac{2}{7} \times \dfrac{21}{32}$

Problem Solving REAL WORLD

13. Amber has a $\dfrac{4}{5}$-pound bag of colored sand. She uses $\dfrac{1}{2}$ of the bag for an art project. How much sand does she use for the project?

14. Tyler has $\dfrac{3}{4}$ month to write a book report. He finished the report in $\dfrac{2}{3}$ that time. How much time did it take Tyler to write the report?

_____

_____

Lesson 37
COMMON CORE STANDARD CC.6.NS.5

Lesson Objective: Understand positive and negative numbers, and use them to represent real-world quantities.

Understand Positive and Negative Numbers

Positive integers are to the right of 0 on the number line.
Negative integers are to the left of 0 on the number line.
Opposites are the same distance from 0, on opposite sides.

What is the opposite of ⁻3?

Step 1 Graph the integer.

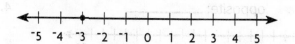

⁻3 is a negative integer. Graph it to the left of 0.

Step 2 Graph the integer and its opposite on a number line.

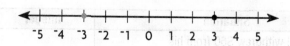

The opposite of ⁻3 is 3 places to the right of 0.

So, the opposite of ⁻3 is 3.

Graph the integer and its opposite on the number line.

1. 2   opposite: _____

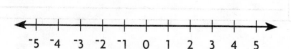

2. ⁻4   opposite: _____

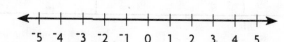

3. ⁻1   opposite: _____

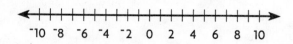

4. 7   opposite: _____

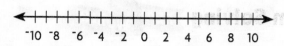

Write the opposite of the opposite of the integer.

5. ⁻18 _____

6. 90 _____

7. ⁻31 _____

The Number System

Understand Positive and Negative Numbers

Graph the integer and its opposite on a number line.

1. ⁻6   opposite: ___⁺6___

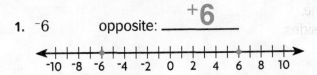

2. 3   opposite: _____

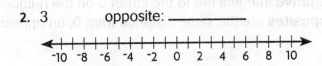

3. 10   opposite: _____

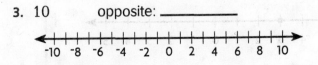

4. ⁻8   opposite: _____

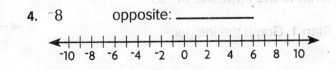

Name the integer that represents the situation, and tell what 0 represents in that situation.

Situation	Integer	What Does 0 Represent?
5. Michael withdrew $60 from his checking account.		
6. Raquel gained 12 points while playing a video game.		
7. Juan went up 25 feet during a climb on a rock climbing wall.		

Write the opposite of the opposite of the integer.

8. ⁻20 _____   9. 4 _____   10. 95 _____   11. ⁻63 _____

Problem Solving  REAL WORLD

12. Dakshesh won a game by scoring 25 points. Randy scored the opposite number of points as Dakshesh. What is Randy's score?

13. When Dakshesh and Randy played the game again, Dakshesh scored the opposite of the opposite of his first score. What is his score?

_____

_____

74

Rational Numbers and the Number Line

Graph ⁻0.8 and 1.3 on the number line.

Step 1 Use positive and negative integers to help you locate the decimals. 0.8 is between 0 and 1, so ⁻0.8 is between 0 and ⁻1. 1.3 is between 1 and 2.

Step 2 The number line is marked in tenths. There is a tick mark every 0.1. Count 8 tick marks to the left of 0 for ⁻0.8. Count 3 tickmarks to the right of 1 for 1.3.

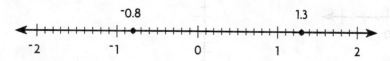

Graph $\frac{3}{5}$ and $^-1\frac{1}{2}$ on the number line.

Step 1 Use positive and negative integers to help you locate the fractions. $\frac{3}{5}$ is between 0 and 1. $1\frac{1}{2}$ is between 1 and 2, so $^-1\frac{1}{2}$ is between ⁻1 and ⁻2.

Step 2 The number line is marked in tenths. There is a tick mark every $\frac{1}{10}$. Use equivalent fractions to help you graph the points.

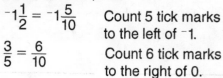

$^-1\frac{1}{2} = ^-1\frac{5}{10}$ Count 5 tick marks to the left of ⁻1.

$\frac{3}{5} = \frac{6}{10}$ Count 6 tick marks to the right of 0.

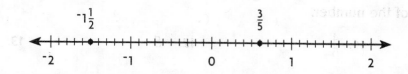

Graph the number on the horizontal number line.

1. $^-1\frac{2}{5}$ **2.** 0.6   **3.** ⁻1.2   **4.** $1\frac{8}{10}$

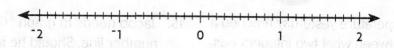

The Number System

Rational Numbers and the Number Line

Graph the number on the number line.

1. $-2\frac{3}{4}$

The number is between the integers ____ and ____.

It is closer to the integer ____.

2. $-\frac{1}{4}$

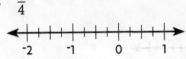

3. -0.5

4. 1.75

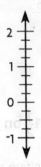

5. $1\frac{1}{2}$

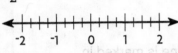

State whether the numbers are on the same or opposite sides of zero.

6. -2.4 and 2.3

7. $-2\frac{1}{5}$ and -1

8. -0.3 and 0.3

9. 0.44 and $-\frac{2}{3}$

_____   _____   _____   _____

Write the opposite of the number.

10. -5.23

11. $\frac{4}{5}$

12. -5

13. $-2\frac{2}{3}$

_____   _____   _____   _____

Problem Solving REAL WORLD

14. The outdoor temperature yesterday reached a low of $-4.5°F$. Between what two integers was the temperature?

15. Jacob needs to graph $-6\frac{2}{5}$ on a horizontal number line. Should he graph it to the left or right of -6?

_____   _____

Lesson 39

COMMON CORE STANDARD CC.6.NS.6b
Lesson Objective: Identify the relationship
between points on a coordinate plane.

Ordered Pair Relationships

You can tell which quadrant to graph a point in by
looking at whether the coordinates are positive or negative.

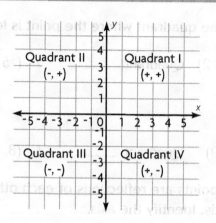

Find the quadrant for the point (4, ⁻5).

Step 1 The x-coordinate is 4, a positive number.
So, the point must be in Quadrant I or IV.

Step 2 The y-coordinate is ⁻5, a negative number.
So, the point must be in Quadrant III or IV.

Step 3 The only quadrant that the x- and y-coordinates
have in common is Quadrant IV.

So, the point (4, ⁻5) is in Quadrant IV.

**Two points are reflections of each other if the x-axis
or y-axis forms a line of symmetry for the two points.
This means that if you folded the graph along that axis,
the two points would line up.**

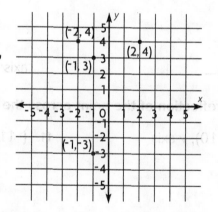

(⁻1, 3) and (⁻1, ⁻3) are reflected across the x-axis.
The x-coordinates are the same. The y-coordinates
are opposites.

(2, 4) and (⁻2, 4) are reflected across the y-axis.
The y-coordinates are the same. The x-coordinates
are opposites.

Identify the quadrant where the point is located.

1. (⁻1, 5)

x-coordinate: ⁻1 Quadrant: _____ or _____

y-coordinate: 5 Quadrant: _____ or _____

The point is in Quadrant _____ .

2. (⁻3, ⁻2)

x-coordinate: ⁻3 Quadrant: _____ or _____

y-coordinate: ⁻2 Quadrant: _____ or _____

The point is in Quadrant _____ .

3. (2, 4)

Quadrant: _____

4. (⁻6, 7)

Quadrant: _____

5. (8, ⁻1)

Quadrant: _____

6. (⁻7, ⁻5)

Quadrant: _____

**The two points are reflections of each other across the x- or y-axis.
Identify the axis.**

7. (2, 7) and (⁻2, 7)

axis: _____

8. (⁻1, 4) and (⁻1, ⁻4)

axis: _____

9. (5, ⁻6) and (5, 6)

axis: _____

10. (8, ⁻3) and (⁻8, ⁻3)

axis: _____

The Number System

Ordered Pair Relationships

Identify the quadrant where the point is located.

1. (10, ⁻2)   Quadrant: __IV__

2. (⁻5, ⁻6)   Quadrant: _____

3. (3, 7)   Quadrant: _____

4. (⁻4, 9)   Quadrant: _____

5. (8, ⁻1)   Quadrant: _____

6. (⁻11, 6)   Quadrant: _____

**The two points are reflections of each other across the
x- or y-axis. Identify the axis.**

7. (5, 3) and (⁻5, 3)

8. (⁻7, 1) and (⁻7, ⁻1)

9. (⁻2, 4) and (⁻2, ⁻4)

axis: _____

axis: _____

axis: _____

Give the reflection of the point across the given axis.

10. (⁻6, ⁻10), y-axis

11. (⁻11, 3), x-axis

12. (8, 2), x-axis

_____

_____

_____

Problem Solving  REAL WORLD

13. A town's post office is located at the point
(7, 5) on a coordinate plane. In which quadrant
is the post office located?

14. The grocery store is located at a point on a
coordinate plane with the same y-coordinate
as the bank but with the opposite x-coordinate.
The grocery store and bank are reflections of
each other across which axis?

_____

_____

Name _____

Fractions and Decimals

Terminating decimals end. **Repeating decimals** do not end but have repeating digits. One way to convert a terminating decimal to a fraction or mixed number is to read the number.

Look at the decimal 5.75. The right-hand digit is in the hundredths place. Read 5.75 as "five and seventy-five hundredths."

whole number ⟶ $5\frac{75}{100}$ ⟵ fraction

As a mixed number, the whole number is 5. The numerator is 75. The denominator is 100.

Write the fraction in simplest form using the greatest common factor.

75: 1, 3, ⑤ 15, ㉕ 75
100: 1, 2, 4, ⑤ 10, 20, ㉕ 50, 100
GCF = 25

$$5\frac{75}{100} = 5\frac{75 \div 25}{100 \div 25} = 5\frac{3}{4}$$

So, 5.75 = $5\frac{3}{4}$ in simplest form.

Identify the decimal and the fraction in simplest form for point E.

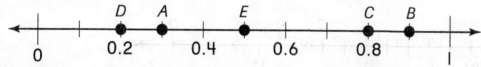

Decimal
Between 0 and 1 there are 10 spaces. So, each space represents 0.1. Point E is one space to the right of 0.4. Point E is the next tenth, or 0.5.

So, Point E is at 0.5 = $\frac{1}{2}$.

Fraction
Read 0.5 as "five-tenths." Write $\frac{5}{10}$. Simplify by dividing the numerator and denominator by the GCF, 5.
$$\frac{5 \div 5}{10 \div 5} = \frac{1}{2}$$

Write as a fraction or mixed number in simplest form.

1. 0.48

2. 0.8

3. 0.004

4. 3.6

5. 4.82

_____ _____ _____ _____ _____

Identify a decimal and a fraction or mixed number in simplest form for each point.

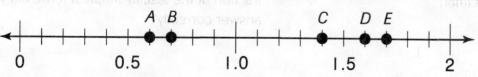

6. Point A

7. Point B

8. Point C

9. Point D

10. Point E

_____ _____ _____ _____ _____

The Number System

Fractions and Decimals

Write as a fraction or as a mixed number in simplest form.

1. 0.52

$$0.52 = \frac{52}{100}$$

$$= \frac{52 \div 4}{100 \div 4} = \frac{13}{25}$$

_____

2. 0.02

_____

3. 4.8

_____

4. 6.025

_____

Write as a decimal. Tell whether the decimal terminates or repeats.

5. $\frac{17}{25}$

_____

6. $\frac{7}{9}$

_____

7. $4\frac{13}{20}$

_____

8. $7\frac{8}{11}$

_____

Identify a decimal and a fraction or mixed number in simplest form for each point.

9. Point A

_____

10. Point D

_____

11. Point C

_____

12. Point B

_____

Problem Solving REAL WORLD

13. Grace sold $\frac{5}{8}$ of her stamp collection. What is this amount as a decimal?

_____

14. What if you scored a 0.80 on a test? What fraction of the test, in simplest form, did you answer correctly?

_____

Compare and Order Fractions and Decimals

You can compare fractions and decimals by rewriting them so all are fractions or decimals.

Use < or > to compare 0.77 and $\frac{7}{10}$.

Method 1

Write the fraction as a decimal.
Then compare the decimals.

$$\frac{7}{10} = 10\overline{)7.0} \begin{array}{c} 0.7 \\ -7.0 \\ \hline 0 \end{array} = 0.7$$

0.77 > 0.7

So, $0.77 > \frac{7}{10}$.

Method 2

Write the decimal as a fraction.
Rewrite $\frac{7}{10}$ with a denominator of 100.
Then compare the fractions.

$$0.77 = \frac{77}{100} \qquad \frac{7}{10} = \frac{7 \times 10}{10 \times 10} = \frac{70}{100}$$

77 > 70

So, $\frac{77}{100} > \frac{70}{100}$ and $0.77 > \frac{7}{10}$.

Order 0.08, $\frac{1}{20}$, and 0.06 from least to greatest.

Write each number as a fraction.

$$0.08 = \frac{8}{100} \qquad \frac{1}{20} = \frac{1}{20} \qquad 0.06 = \frac{6}{100}$$

Compare the fractions.

Compare the fractions with the same denominator.

8 > 6

So, $\frac{8}{100} > \frac{6}{100}$.

Compare the fractions with different denominators using common denominators.

$$\frac{1}{20} = \frac{1 \times 5}{20 \times 5} = \frac{5}{100}, \; 5 < 6, \text{ so } \frac{1}{20} < \frac{6}{100}.$$

So, $\frac{1}{20} < \frac{6}{100} < \frac{8}{100}$.

So, the numbers from least to greatest are $\frac{1}{20}$, 0.06, and 0.08.

Compare. Write <, >, or = in each ◯.

1. $\frac{4}{11}$ ◯ $\frac{2}{11}$

2. $\frac{5}{7}$ ◯ $\frac{5}{6}$

3. 0.27 ◯ 0.3

4. 0.9 ◯ $\frac{4}{25}$

Order from least to greatest.

5. $\frac{3}{8}$, $\frac{5}{16}$, $\frac{1}{4}$

6. 0.7, 0.82, $\frac{4}{5}$

7. $2\frac{1}{6}$, $1\frac{5}{12}$, $2\frac{1}{4}$

8. 0.64, 0.6, $\frac{5}{8}$, 0.59

Compare and Order Fractions and Decimals

Write <, >, or =.

1. $0.64 \enspace \boxed{<} \enspace \dfrac{7}{10}$

   $0.64 < 0.7$

2. $0.48 \enspace \bigcirc \enspace \dfrac{6}{15}$

3. $0.75 \enspace \bigcirc \enspace \dfrac{7}{8}$

4. $7\dfrac{1}{8} \enspace \bigcirc \enspace 7.025$

Order from least to greatest.

5. $\dfrac{7}{12}, \enspace 0.75, \enspace \dfrac{5}{6}$

6. $0.5, \enspace 0.41, \enspace \dfrac{3}{5}$

7. $3.25, \enspace 3\dfrac{2}{5}, \enspace 3\dfrac{3}{8}$

8. $0.9, \enspace \dfrac{8}{9}, \enspace 0.86$

_____

Order from greatest to least.

9. $0.7, \enspace \dfrac{7}{9}, \enspace \dfrac{7}{8}$

10. $0.2, \enspace 0.19, \enspace \dfrac{3}{5}$

11. $6\dfrac{1}{20}, \enspace 6.1, \enspace 6.07$

12. $2\dfrac{1}{2}, \enspace 2.4, \enspace 2.35, \enspace 2\dfrac{1}{8}$

_____

Problem Solving REAL WORLD

13. One day it snowed $3\dfrac{3}{8}$ inches in Altoona and 3.45 inches in Bethlehem. Which city received less snow that day?

    _____

14. Malia and John each bought 2 pounds of sunflower seeds. Each ate some seeds. Malia has $1\dfrac{1}{3}$ pounds left, and John has $1\dfrac{2}{5}$ pounds left. Who ate more sunflower seeds?

    _____

© Houghton Mifflin Harcourt Publishing Company

Name _____

Lesson 42

COMMON CORE STANDARD CC.6.NS.6c

Lesson Objective: Plot ordered pairs of
rational numbers on a coordinate plane.

Rational Numbers and the Coordinate Plane

A **coordinate plane** is formed by two intersecting lines on a grid. The horizontal line is the *x*-axis. The vertical line is the *y*-axis. They intersect at the **origin**.

An **ordered pair** shows the horizontal and vertical distances a point is from the origin. Positive numbers in an ordered pair mean "right" for the first number and "up" for the second number. Negative numbers mean "left" for the first number and "down" for the second number.

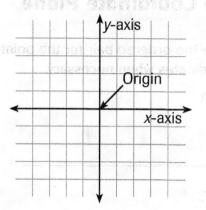

Write the ordered pair for point *K*.

Step 1 Place your finger at point *K*. Place your pencil tip at the origin.

Step 2 With your pencil tip, count how many units to the right or left of the origin point *K* is. Record that number.

   Point *K* is 2.5 units right of the origin, so the first number in the ordered pair is ⁺2.5, or 2.5.

Step 3 With your pencil tip, count how many units down from the origin point *K* is. Record that number.

   Point *K* is 3.5 units down from the origin, so the second number in the ordered pair is ⁻3.5.

So, the ordered pair for point *K* is (2.5, ⁻3.5).

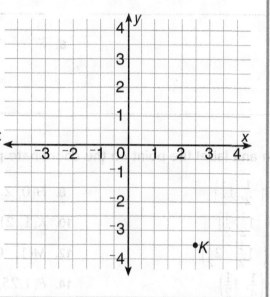

Write the ordered pair for each point.

1. point *P* _____

2. point *Q* _____

3. point *R* _____

4. point *S* _____

5. point *T* _____

6. point *U* _____

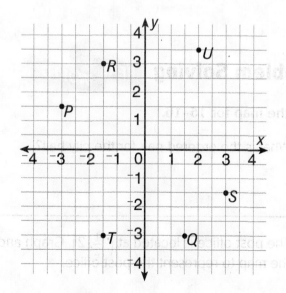

The Number System

Name _____

Lesson 42

CC.6.NS.6c

Rational Numbers and the Coordinate Plane

Write the ordered pair for the point. Give approximate coordinates when necessary.

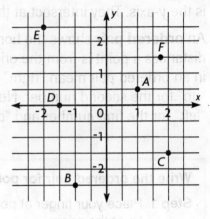

1. *A*

$$\left(1, \frac{1}{2}\right)$$

_____

2. *B*

_____

3. *C*

_____

4. *D*

_____

5. *E*

_____

6. *F*

_____

Graph and label the point on the coordinate plane.

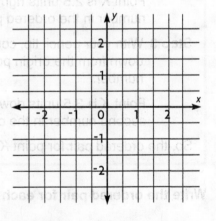

7. $G\left(-\frac{1}{2}, 1\frac{1}{2}\right)$

8. $H(0, 2.50)$

9. $J\left(-1\frac{1}{2}, \frac{1}{2}\right)$

10. $K(1, 2)$

11. $L\left(-1\frac{1}{2}, -2\frac{1}{2}\right)$

12. $M(1, -0.5)$

13. $N\left(\frac{1}{4}, 1\frac{1}{2}\right)$

14. $P(1.25, 0)$

Problem Solving REAL WORLD

Use the map for 15–16.

15. What is the ordered pair for the city hall?

_____

16. The post office is located at $\left(-\frac{1}{2}, 2\right)$. Graph and label a point on the map to represent the post office.

Map of Elmwood

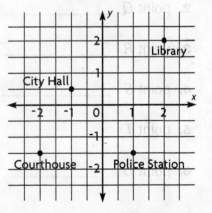

© Houghton Mifflin Harcourt Publishing Company

84

Compare and Order Integers

Use a number line to compare ⁻2 and ⁻4.

Step 1 Graph ⁻2 and ⁻4. Both numbers are negative integers.
Graph them to the left of 0.

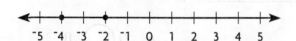

⁻5 ⁻4 ⁻3 ⁻2 ⁻1 0 1 2 3 4 5

Step 2 Decide which number is greater. Numbers become greater
as you move to the right on a number line.

⁻2 is to the right of ⁻4.

So, ⁻2 is greater than ⁻4. Write: ⁻2 > ⁻4.

Order these integers from least to greatest: 3, ⁻7, 0, 4, ⁻1.

Step 1 Graph the integers on a number line.

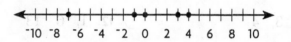

⁻10 ⁻8 ⁻6 ⁻4 ⁻2 0 2 4 6 8 10

Step 2 Write the numbers in order from left (least) to right (greatest).   ⁻7, ⁻1, 0, 3, 4

Compare the numbers. Write < or >.

1. 3 ◯ ⁻6

⁻10 ⁻8 ⁻6 ⁻4 ⁻2 0 2 4 6 8 10

3 is to the _____ of ⁻6 on the number line,
so 3 is _____ than ⁻6.

2. ⁻4 ◯ 2   **3.** 1 ◯ ⁻5   **4.** ⁻7 ◯ ⁻3

Order the numbers from least to greatest.

5. 4, ⁻3, ⁻5   **6.** ⁻11, 2, 6   **7.** 8, ⁻7, 4

____ < ____ < ____   ____ < ____ < ____   ____ < ____ < ____

Order the numbers from greatest to least.

8. 1, ⁻2, 0   **9.** ⁻6, 2, 5   **10.** ⁻3, 3, ⁻4

____ > ____ > ____   ____ > ____ > ____   ____ > ____ > ____

Compare and Order Integers

Compare the numbers. Write < or >.

1. ⁻4 ⟩ ⁻5   Think: ⁻4 is to the ___right___ of ⁻5 on the number line,

   so ⁻4 is ___greater than___ ⁻5.

2. 0 ◯ ⁻1

3. 4 ◯ ⁻6

4. ⁻9 ◯ ⁻8

5. 2 ◯ ⁻10

6. ⁻12 ◯ ⁻11

7. 1 ◯ ⁻10

Order the numbers from least to greatest.

8. 3, ⁻2, ⁻7

9. 0, 2, ⁻5

10. ⁻9, ⁻12, ⁻10

____ < ____ < ____   ____ < ____ < ____   ____ < ____ < ____

11. ⁻2, ⁻3, ⁻4

12. 1, ⁻6, ⁻13

13. 5, 7, 0

____ < ____ < ____   ____ < ____ < ____   ____ < ____ < ____

Order the numbers from greatest to least.

14. 0, 13, ⁻13

15. ⁻11, 7, ⁻5

16. ⁻9, ⁻8, 1

____ > ____ > ____   ____ > ____ > ____   ____ > ____ > ____

17. 32, 10, ⁻22

18. ⁻2, ⁻4, 0

19. ⁻25, 19, 26

____ > ____ > ____   ____ > ____ > ____   ____ > ____ > ____

Problem Solving REAL WORLD

20. Meg and Derek played a game. Meg scored
    ⁻11 points, and Derek scored 4 points. Write
    a comparison to show that Meg's score is less
    than Derek's score.

21. Misha is thinking of a negative integer
    greater than ⁻4. What number could she
    be thinking of?

_____   _____

Name _____

Compare and Order Rational Numbers

Compare 0.5 and ⁻3 using the number line.

Step 1 Graph the numbers. Use positive and negative integers to help you locate the decimals.
0.5 is between 0 and 1.
⁻3 is negative, so it is to the left of 0.

Step 2 As you move right on the number line, numbers become greater.

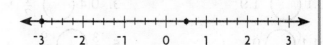

So, 0.5 > ⁻3.

Compare ⁻2$\frac{1}{4}$ and 1$\frac{1}{2}$ using the number line.

Step 1 Graph the numbers. Use positive and negative integers to help you locate the fractions.
⁻2$\frac{1}{4}$ is between ⁻2 and ⁻3. 1$\frac{1}{2}$ is between 1 and 2.

Step 2 As you move left on the number line, numbers become less.

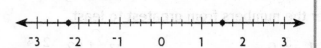

So, ⁻2$\frac{1}{4}$ < 1$\frac{1}{2}$.

Compare the numbers. Write < or >.

1. ⁻0.7 ◯ ⁻1$\frac{1}{8}$ **2.** 0.3 ◯ ⁻4.6   **3.** ⁻$\frac{1}{4}$ ◯ 3.2   **4.** ⁻$\frac{5}{8}$ ◯ ⁻2$\frac{1}{2}$

Order the numbers from least to greatest.

5. 1.3, ⁻4$\frac{1}{5}$, ⁻$\frac{1}{2}$ **6.** ⁻2.5, ⁻0.9, 1   **7.** 2, 2$\frac{2}{3}$, ⁻3.2

____ < ____ < ____   ____ < ____ < ____   ____ < ____ < ____

The Number System

Name _____

Compare and Order Rational Numbers

Compare the numbers. Write < or >.

1. $-1\frac{1}{2}$ $\bigcirc<$ $-\frac{1}{2}$ Think: $-1\frac{1}{2}$ is to the ___left___ of $-\frac{1}{2}$ on the number line,

    so $-1\frac{1}{2}$ is ___less than___ $-\frac{1}{2}$.

2. 0.1 $\bigcirc$ -1.9

3. 0.4 $\bigcirc$ $-\frac{1}{2}$

4. $\frac{2}{5}$ $\bigcirc$ 0.5

5. -1.1 $\bigcirc$ 0

6. $\frac{3}{4}$ $\bigcirc$ $\frac{9}{10}$

7. -2.5 $\bigcirc$ $-\frac{3}{1}$

Order the numbers from least to greatest.

8. 0.2, -1.7, -1

9. $-2\frac{3}{4}$, $-\frac{3}{5}$, $-1\frac{3}{4}$

10. -0.5, $-1\frac{2}{3}$, -2.7

_____ < _____ < _____   _____ < _____ < _____   _____ < _____ < _____

Order the numbers from greatest to least.

11. -1, $-\frac{5}{6}$, 0

12. 1.82, $-\frac{2}{5}$, $\frac{4}{5}$

13. -2.19, -2.5, 1.1

_____ > _____ < _____   _____ > _____ > _____   _____ > _____ > _____

Write a comparison using < or > to show the relationship between the two values.

14. an elevation of -15 m and an elevation of -20.5 m

15. a balance of $78 and a balance of $-$42

16. a score of -31 points and a score of -30 points

_____   _____   _____

Problem Solving REAL WORLD

17. The temperature in Cold Town on Monday was 1°C. The temperature in Frosty Town on Monday was -2°C. Which town was colder on Monday?

18. Stan's bank account balance is less than $-$20.00 but greater than $-$21.00. What could Stan's account balance be?

_____   _____

Lesson 45

COMMON CORE STANDARD CC.6.NS.7c

Lesson Objective: Find and interpret the absolute value of rational numbers.

Absolute Value

Absolute value is a number's distance from 0 on a number line.
Numbers and their opposites have the same absolute value.

Find the absolute value of ⁻3 and 4.

Step 1 Graph the numbers.

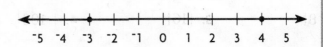

Step 2 Find each number's distance from 0.

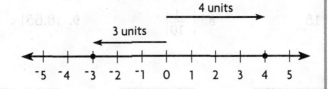

Step 3 Write the absolute value. $|{-3}| = 3$ $|4| = 4$

Find the absolute value of ⁻0.75 and 2.25.

Step 1 Graph the numbers.

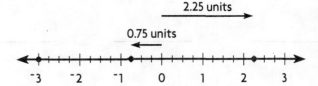

Step 2 Find each number's distance from 0.

Step 3 Write the absolute value. $|{-0.75}| = 0.75$ $|2.25| = 2.25$

Find the absolute value.

1. $\left|{-3\frac{2}{3}}\right|$ $-3\frac{2}{3}$ is _____ units from 0.

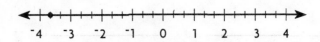

   $\left|{-3\frac{2}{3}}\right| =$ ___

2. $|{-2.5}| =$ _____   3. $|7| =$ _____   4. $\left|\frac{4}{10}\right| =$ ___   5. $|{-1}| =$ _____   6. $\left|{-1\frac{4}{5}}\right| =$ ___

Name _____

Absolute Value

Find the absolute value.

1. $|7|$ Graph 7 on the number line.

   7 is ___**7**___ units from 0.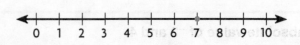

   $|7| =$ ___**7**___

2. $|-8|$ 3. $|16|$ 4. $|-100|$ 5. $|0|$ 6. $|-5,000|$

_____   _____   _____   _____   _____

7. $|-15|$ 8. $\left|-\dfrac{1}{10}\right|$ 9. $|8.65|$ 10. $\left|4\dfrac{3}{20}\right|$ 11. $|-0.06|$

_____   _____   _____   _____   _____

Find all numbers with the given absolute value.

12. 12   13. 1.7   14. $\dfrac{3}{5}$ 15. $3\dfrac{1}{6}$ 16. 0

_____   _____   _____   _____   _____

_____   _____   _____   _____   _____

Find the number or numbers that make the statement true.

17. $\left|\right| = 17$ 18. $\left|\right| = 2.04$ 19. $\left|\right| = 1\dfrac{9}{10}$ 20. $\left|\right| = \dfrac{19}{24}$

_____   _____   _____   _____

_____   _____   _____   _____

Problem Solving REAL WORLD

21. Which two numbers are 7.5 units away from 0 on a number line?

22. Emilio is playing a game. He just answered a question incorrectly, so his score will change by -10 points. Find the absolute value of -10.

_____   _____

Compare Absolute Values

Use absolute value to express an elevation less than ⁻10 meters as a depth.

Step 1 Elevation indicates distance from sea level.
A negative elevation means a distance below sea level.
⁻10 is 10 units below 0 on the vertical number line. This shows that the absolute value of ⁻10 is 10.

Step 2 Depth indicates distance below sea level.
It is always expressed as a positive number.
Use the absolute value of ⁻10 to find the depth: $|{-}10| = 10$

Step 3 List three elevations that are less than ⁻10 meters. Write the corresponding depths.

Elevation (m)	Depth (m)
⁻15	15
⁻20	20
⁻30	30

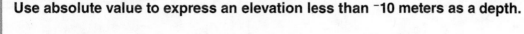

So, an elevation less than ⁻10 meters is a depth greater than 10 meters.

Complete the table.

1.

Elevations Greater than ⁻13	Depth
⁻12 feet	12 feet
⁻8 feet	
	2 feet

2. Jordin's savings account balance is greater than ⁻$27. Use absolute value to describe the balance as a debt.

Jordin's balance is a debt of _____ than $27.

3. The table shows the changes in the weights of 3 dogs. Which dog had the greatest decrease in weight? How much weight did the dog lose?

_____

Dog	Weight Change (lb)
Duffy	1.3
Buddy	⁻1.1
Dinah	⁻1.4

The Number System

Compare Absolute Values

Solve.

1. Jamie scored ⁻5 points on her turn at a trivia game. In Veronica's turn, she scored more points than Jamie. Use absolute value to describe Veronica's score as a loss.

   In this situation, |⁻5| represents a loss of ____5____ points. Veronica lost __fewer__ than 5 points.

2. The low temperature on Friday was ⁻10°F. The low temperature on Saturday was colder. Use absolute value to describe the temperature on Saturday as a temperature below zero.

   The temperature on Saturday was _____ than 10 degrees below zero.

3. The table shows changes in the savings accounts of five students. Which student had the greatest increase in money? By how much did the student's account increase?

   _____

   _____

Student	Account Change ($)
Brett	⁻12
Destiny	⁻36
Carissa	15
Rylan	10

Compare. Write <, >, or =.

4. ⁻16 ◯ |⁻16|

5. 20 ◯ |20|

6. 3 ◯ |⁻4|

7. |⁻12| ◯ |⁻11|

8. |25| ◯ |27|

9. |⁻9| ◯ |9|

Problem Solving · REAL WORLD

10. On Wednesday, Miguel's bank account balance was ⁻$55. On Thursday, his balance was less than that. Use absolute value to describe Miguel's balance on Thursday as a debt.

    In this situation, ⁻$55 represents a debt of

    _____. On Thursday, Miguel had a debt

    of _____ than $55.

11. During a game, Naomi lost points. She lost fewer than 3 points. Use an integer to describe her possible score.

    _____

Name _____

Lesson **47**

COMMON CORE STANDARD CC.6.NS.8
Lesson Objective: Find horizontal and
vertical distances on the coordinate plane.

Distance on the Coordinate Plane

Find the distance between (4, ⁻2) and (4, 3).

Step 1 Graph the points. Points with the same
x-coordinate are on the same vertical line.
Think of the vertical line as a number line
that shows the *y*-coordinates.

Step 2 Use absolute value to find the distances
between the *y*-coordinates and 0.

|⁻2| shows the distance from ⁻2 to 0.
|⁻2| = 2 units
|3| shows the distance from 3 to 0.
|⁻3| = 3 units

Step 3 Since the points are in different quadrants,
add to find the total distance between the
y-coordinates.

So, the distance between (4, ⁻2) and (4, 3) is 5 units.

Use the same steps when two points have the same *y*-coordinates.
Find the distance between the *x*-coordinates to find the distance
between the points.

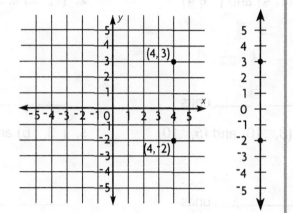

Graph the pair of points. Then find the distance between them.

1. (4, ⁻4) and (1, ⁻4)

The points are on the same horizontal line.

Distance from 4 to 0: _____ = _____

Distance from 1 to 0: _____ = _____

Subtract to find distance from (4, ⁻4) to (1, ⁻4):

_____ − _____ = _____ units

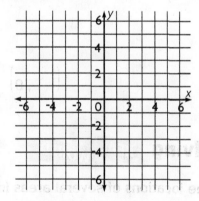

2. (2, ⁻5) and (2, 3)

_____ units

3. (⁻1, 3) and (5, 3)

_____ units

4. (⁻6, 1) and (⁻6, ⁻2)

_____ units

The Number System

Distance on the Coordinate Plane

Find the distance between the pair of points.

1. (1, 4) and (⁻3, 4)

$$|1| = 1; |^-3| = 3;$$
$$1 + 3 = 4$$

_____ 4 _____ units

2. (7, ⁻2) and (11, ⁻2)

_____ units

3. (6, 4) and (6, ⁻8)

_____ units

4. (8, ⁻10) and (5, ⁻10)

_____ units

5. (⁻2, ⁻6) and (⁻2, 5)

_____ units

6. (⁻5, 2) and (⁻5, ⁻4)

_____ units

Write the coordinates of a point that is the given distance from the given point.

7. 5 units from (⁻1, ⁻2)

8. 8 units from (2, 4)

9. 3 units from (⁻7, ⁻5)

 (, ⁻2)

 (2,)

 (⁻7,)

10. 6 units from (4, ⁻1)

11. 10 units from (⁻1, 9)

12. 7 units from (⁻3, 2)

(4,)

(, 9)

(, 2)

Problem Solving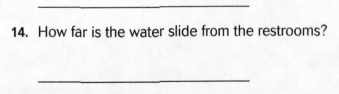

The map shows the locations of several areas in an amusement park. Each unit represents 1 kilometer.

13. How far is the Ferris wheel from the rollercoaster?

_____

14. How far is the water slide from the restrooms?

_____

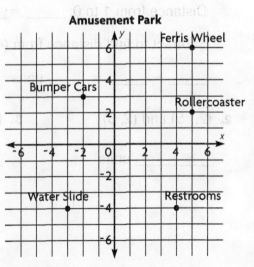

Amusement Park

Name _____

Problem Solving • The Coordinate Plane

Lesson 48
COMMON CORE STANDARD CC.6.NS.8
Lesson Objective: Solve problems on the coordinate plane by using the strategy *draw a diagram*.

Zachary is drawing a coordinate map of his town. He has graphed the police station at the point (2, ¯1). He is going to place the library 4 units up from the police station. What ordered pair shows where he will graph the library?

Read the Problem		
What do I need to find? I need to find the _____ for the library.	**What information do I need to use?** The ordered pair for the _____ is _____. The library is _____ units _____ from the police station.	**How will I use the information?** I can draw a diagram to _____ the information on a coordinate plane.

Solve the Problem
Graph the point _____.   Label it _____.   From this point, count _____ units _____   Graph the new point, and label it _____.   So, the ordered pair for the library will be _____.

Solve. Graph the pairs of points on the coordinate plane.

1. Zachary has graphed the middle school at (¯6, 5). He has graphed the high school 3 units to the right of the middle school. What is the high school's ordered pair?

   _____

2. Zachary will graph the apartment building 2 units to the left and 5 units down from the grocery store. He has graphed the grocery store at (7, 8). Give the ordered pair for the apartment building.

   _____

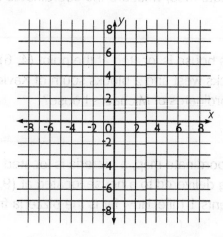

© Houghton Mifflin Harcourt Publishing Company

The Number System

95

Problem Solving • The Coordinate Plane

Read each problem and solve.

1. On a coordinate map of Clifton, an electronics store is located
   at (6, ‾7). A convenience store is located 7 units north of the
   electronics store on the map. What are the map coordinates of
   the convenience store?

   (6, 0)

2. Sonya and Lucas walk from the school to the library. They walk
   5 blocks south and 4 blocks west to get to the library. If the
   school is located at a point (9, ‾1) on a coordinate map, what
   are the map coordinates of the library?

   _____

3. On a coordinate map, Sherry's house is at the point
   (10, ‾2) and the mall is at point (‾4, ‾2). If each unit on
   the map represents one block, what is the distance between
   Sherry's house and the mall?

   _____

4. Arthur left his job at (5, 4) on a coordinate map and walked to
   his house at (5, ‾6). Each unit on the map represents 1 block.
   How far did Arthur walk?

   _____

5. A fire station is located 2 units east and 6 units north of a
   hospital. If the hospital is located at a point (‾2, ‾3) on a
   coordinate map, what are the coordinates of the fire station?

   _____

6. Xavier's house is located at the point (4, 6). Michael's house is
   10 blocks west and 2 blocks south of Xavier's house. What are
   the coordinates of Michael's house?

   _____

7. On a coordinate map, a pizzeria is located at (9, 3). A pizza
   is being delivered to a house located at (9, ‾3). Each unit
   represents 1 mile. How far is the pizzeria from the house?

   _____

Exponents

An **exponent** tells how many times a number is used as a factor.

The **base** is the number being multiplied repeatedly.

For example, in 2^5, 5 is the exponent and 2 is the base.

$2^5 = 2 \times 2 \times 2 \times 2 \times 2 = 32$

Write the expression 4^5 using equal factors. Then find the value.

Step 1 Identify the base.	The base is 4.
Step 2 Identify the exponent.	The exponent is 5.
Step 3 Write the base as many times as the exponent tells you. Place a multiplication symbol between the bases.	$4 \times 4 \times 4 \times 4 \times 4$ You should have one less multiplication symbol than the value of the exponent.
Step 4 Multiply.	$4 \times 4 \times 4 \times 4 \times 4 = 1{,}024$

So, $4^5 = 1{,}024$.

Write as an expression using equal factors. Then find the value.

1. 3^4

2. 2^6

3. 4^3

4. 5^3

5. 10^4

6. 8^5

7. 11^4

8. 15^2

9. 10^7

10. 25^4

Expressions and Equations

Exponents

Use one or more exponents to write the expression.

1. 6×6

2. $11 \times 11 \times 11 \times 11$

3. $9 \times 9 \times 9 \times 9 \times 7 \times 7$

6^2

_____

Find the value.

4. 9^2

5. 6^4

6. 1^6

_____

7. 5^3

8. 10^5

9. 23^2

_____

10. Write 144 with an exponent by using 12 as the base.

11. Write 343 with an exponent by using 7 as the base.

_____

_____

Problem Solving  REAL WORLD

12. Each day Sheila doubles the number of push-ups she did the day before. On the fifth day, she does $2 \times 2 \times 2 \times 2 \times 2$ push-ups. Use an exponent to write the number of push-ups Shelia does on the fifth day.

13. The city of Beijing has a population of more than 10^7 people. Write 10^7 without using an exponent.

_____

_____

Evaluate Expressions Involving Exponents

A **numerical expression** is a mathematical phrase that includes only numbers and operation symbols.

You **evaluate** the expression when you perform all the computations.

To evaluate an expression, use the **order of operations.**

Order of Operations
1. Parentheses
2. Exponents
3. Multiply and Divide
4. Add and Subtract

Evaluate the expression $(10 + 6^2) - 4 \times 10$.

Step 1 Start with the *parentheses*. Use the order of operations for the computations inside the parentheses.

$10 + 6^2$
Find the value of the number with an *exponent*. Rewrite as multiplication:
$10 + 6^2 = 10 + 6 \times 6$
Multiply and divide from left to right:
$10 + 6 \times 6 = 10 + 36$
Add and subtract from left to right:
$10 + 36 = 46$

Step 2 Rewrite the original expression, using the value from Step 1 for the part in parentheses.

$(10 + 6^2) - 4 \times 10 = \mathbf{46} - 4 \times 10$

Step 3 Now that the parentheses are cleared, look for *exponents*.

There are no more *exponents*, so go on to the next step in the order of operations.

Step 4 *Multiply and divide* from left to right.

$46 - 4 \times 10 = 46 - 40$

Step 5 *Add and subtract* from left to right.

$46 - 40 = 6$

So, $(10 + 6^2) - 4 \times 10 = 6$.

Evaluate the expression.

1. $8^2 - (7^2 + 1)$

2. $5 - 2^2 + 12 \div 4$

3. $8 \times (16 - 2^4)$

_____

4. $3^2 \times (28 - 20 \div 2)$

5. $(30 - 15 \div 3) \div 5^2$

6. $(6^2 - 3^2) - 9 \div 3$

_____

Expressions and Equations

Evaluate Expressions Involving Exponents

Evaluate the expression.

1. $5 + 17 - 10^2 \div 5$

$5 + 17 - 100 \div 5$
$5 + 17 - 20$
$22 - 20$
2

2. $7^2 - 3^2 + 4$

3. $2^4 \div (7 - 5)$

4. $(8^2 + 36) \div (4 \times 5^2)$

5. $12 + 21 \div 3 + 2^5 \times 0$

6. $(12 - 8)^3 - 24 + 3$

Place parentheses in the expression so that it equals the given value.

7. $12 \times 2 + 2^3$; value: 120

8. $7^2 + 1 - 5 \times 3$; value: 135

Problem Solving  REAL WORLD

9. Hugo is saving for a new baseball glove. He saves $10 the first week, and $6 each week for the next 6 weeks. The expression $10 + 6^2$ represents the total amount in dollars he has saved. What is the total amount Hugo has saved?

10. A scientist placed fish eggs in a tank. Each day, twice the number of eggs from the previous day hatch. The expression 5×2^6 represents the number of eggs that hatch on the sixth day. How many eggs hatch on the sixth day?

Name _____

Write Algebraic Expressions

Word problems use expressions that you can write with symbols. An **algebraic expression** has at least one variable. A **variable** is a letter or symbol that represents one or more numbers. Writing algebraic expressions for words helps you solve word problems.

These are a few common words that are used for operations.

add (+)	subtract (−)	multiply (×)	divide (÷)
sum	difference	product	quotient
increased by	minus	times	divided by
plus	decreased by		
more than	less		
	less than		

17 more than x
$x + 17$

"More than" means add.
"17 more than x" means add 17 to x.

four times the sum of 7 and n
$4 \times (7 + n)$

"Times" means multiply.
"Sum" means add.
The words mean multiply 4 by (7 + n).

A number next to a variable always shows multiplication.
For example, **5n** means the same as **5 × n**.

Write an algebraic expression for the word expression.

1. b divided by 9

2. c more than 5

3. d decreased by 29

4. 8 times g

5. p increased by 12

6. the quotient of k and 14

7. 17 less than the product of 3 and m

8. 2 less than the quotient of d and 16

Write Algebraic Expressions

Write an algebraic expression for the word expression.

1. 13 less than *p*

$$p - 13$$

2. the sum of *x* and 9

_____

3. 6 more than the difference of *b* and 5

_____

4. the sum of 15 and the product of 5 and *v*

_____

5. the difference of 2 and the product of 3 and *k*

_____

6. 12 divided by the sum of *h* and 2

_____

7. the quotient of *m* and 7

_____

8. 9 more than 2 multiplied by *f*

_____

9. 6 minus the difference of *x* and 3

_____

10. 10 less than the quotient of *g* and 3

_____

11. the sum of 4 multiplied by *a* and 5 multiplied by *b*

_____

12. 14 more than the difference of *r* and *s*

_____

Problem Solving

13. Let *h* represent Mark's height in inches. Suzanne is 7 inches shorter than Mark. Write an algebraic expression that represents Suzanne's height in inches.

_____

14. A company rents bicycles for a fee of $10 plus $4 per hour of use. Write an algebraic expression for the total cost in dollars for renting a bicycle for *h* hours.

_____

Name _____

Lesson 52

COMMON CORE STANDARD CC.6.EE.2b
Lesson Objective: Identify and describe parts of expressions.

Identify Parts of Expressions

Each part of an expression between the operation signs + or − is a **term**. A **coefficient** is a number multiplied by a variable, or letter.

Describe the parts of the expression 6b − 7. Then write a word expression.

Step 1 Identify the terms.	There are two terms: 6b and 7.
Step 2 Describe the terms.	The first term shows multiplication: $6b = 6 \times b$ 6b is the product of 6 (the coefficient) and b (the variable). The second term is the number 7.
Step 3 Identify the operation separating the terms.	Subtraction gives the difference of the two terms in the expression.
Step 4 Write a word expression.	"the difference of 6 times b and 7" or "7 less than the product of 6 and b"

Identify the parts of the expression. Then write a word expression for the numerical or algebraic expression.

1. $5 \times (m - 2)$

Identify the parts. _____

Describe the parts. _____

_____

Identify the operations. _____

Write a word expression. _____

2. $12 \div 2 + 7$

_____

_____

_____

_____

3. $8y + (2 \times 11)$

_____

_____

_____

_____

Expressions and Equations

103

Identify Parts of Expressions

Identify the parts of the expression. Then write a word expression for the numerical or algebraic expression.

1. $(16 - 7) \div 3$

The subtraction is the difference
of 16 and 7. The division is the
quotient of the difference and 3.
Word expression: the quotient of
the difference of 16 and 7 and 3

2. $20 + 5 \times 9$

_____
_____
_____
_____

3. $2e - f$

_____
_____
_____
_____

4. $8 + 6q + q$

_____
_____
_____
_____

Identify the terms of the expression. Then give the coefficient of each term.

5. $11r + 7s$

_____
_____

6. $6g - h$

_____
_____

Problem Solving REAL WORLD

7. Adam bought granola bars at the store. The expression $6p + 5n$ gives the number of bars in p boxes of plain granola bars and n boxes of granola bars with nuts. What are the terms of the expression?

_____
_____

8. In the sixth grade, each student will get 4 new books. There is one class of 15 students and one class of 20 students. The expression $4 \times (15 + 20)$ gives the total number of new books. Write a word expression for the numerical expression.

_____
_____

© Houghton Mifflin Harcourt Publishing Company

Evaluate Algebraic Expressions and Formulas

To evaluate an algebraic expression or formula, substitute the value for the variable. Then follow the order of operations.

Evaluate $5x + x^3$ for $x = 3, 2, 1,$ and 0.

$5x + x^3$ for $x = 3$	$5x + x^3$ for $x = 2$	$5x + x^3$ for $x = 1$	$5x + x^3$ for $x = 0$
$5 \times 3 + 3^3$	$5 \times 2 + 2^3$	$5 \times 1 + 1^3$	$5 \times 0 + 0^3$
$5 \times 3 + 27$	$5 \times 2 + 8$	$5 \times 1 + 1$	$5 \times 0 + 0$
$15 + 27$	$10 + 8$	$5 + 1$	$0 + 0$
42	18	6	0

To evaluate an expression with more than one variable, substitute each variable's value. Then follow the order of operations.

Evaluate $4c - 7 + 2d$ for $c = 2$ and $d = 5$.

$4 \times 2 - 7 + 2 \times 5$

$\quad 8 - 7 + 10$

$\qquad 1 + 10$

$\qquad\quad 11$

So, $4c - 7 + 2d = 11$ for $c = 2$ and $d = 5$.

Evaluate the expression for $x = 3, 2, 1,$ and 0.

1. $13 + 6x$ **2.** $5x + 2$ **3.** $2x + 3 + x^2$ **4.** $2x + x^2$

_____ _____ _____ _____

Evaluate the expression for the given values of the variables.

5. $7x + y + 16$ for   **6.** $8a + 11 - 2b$ for   **7.** $12b - 2c + 3$ for
     $x = 2, y = 3$ $a = 4, b = 2$ $b = 5, c = 10$

_____ _____ _____

Evaluate Algebraic Expressions and Formulas

Evaluate the expression for the given values of the variables.

1. $w + 6$ for $w = 11$

$11 + 6$

17

2. $r - 9$ for $r = 20$

_____

3. $17 - 2c$ for $c = 7$

_____

4. $b^2 - 4$ for $b = 5$

_____

5. $(h - 3)^2$ for $h = 5$

_____

6. $x + x^2$ for $x = 6$

_____

7. $m + 2m + 3$ for $m = 12$

_____

8. $9a - 5a$ for $a = 7$

_____

9. $4 \times (21 - 3h)$ for $h = 5$

_____

10. $7m - 9n$ for $m = 7$ and $n = 5$

_____

11. $d^2 - 9k + 3$ for $d = 10$ and $k = 9$

_____

12. $3x + 4y \div 2$ for $x = 7$ and $y = 10$

_____

Problem Solving REAL WORLD

13. The formula $P = 2\ell + 2w$ gives the perimeter P of a rectangular room with length ℓ and width w. A rectangular living room is 26 feet long and 21 feet wide. What is the perimeter of the room?

_____

14. The formula $c = 5(f - 32) \div 9$ gives the Celsius temperature in c degrees for a Fahrenheit temperature of f degrees. What is the Celsius temperature for a Fahrenheit temperature of 122 degrees?

_____

Problem Solving • Combine Like Terms

Use a bar model to solve the problem.

Each hour a company assembles 10 bikes. It sends 6 of those bikes to stores and keeps the rest of the bikes to sell itself. The expression $10h - 6h$ represents the number of bikes the store keeps to sell itself for h hours of work. Simplify the expression by combining like terms.

Read the Problem		
What do I need to find? I need to simplify the expression _____.	**What information do I need to use?** I need to use the like terms $10h$ and _____.	**How will I use the information?** I can use a bar model to find the difference of the _____ terms.

Solve the Problem

Draw a bar model to subtract _____ from _____. Each square represents h, or $1h$.

10 h

h	h	h	h	h	h	h	h	h	h

h	h	h	h	h	h

6 h   _____ h

The model shows that $10h - 6h =$ _____.

So, a simplified expression for the number of bikes the store keeps is _____.

---

1. Bradley sells produce in boxes at a farmer's market. He put 6 ears of corn and 9 tomatoes in each box. The expression $6b + 9b$ represents the total pieces of produce in b boxes. Simplify the expression by combining like terms.

2. Andre bought pencils in packs of 8. He gave 2 pencils to his sister and 3 pencils from each pack to his friends. The expression $8p - 3p - 2$ represents the number of pencils Andre has left from p packs. Simplify the expression by combining like terms.

Problem Solving • Combine Like Terms

Read each problem and solve.

1. A box of pens costs $3 and a box of markers costs $5. The expression $3p + 5p$ represents the cost in dollars to make p packages that includes 1 box of pens and 1 box of markers. Simplify the expression by combining like terms.

$$3p + 5p = 8p$$

2. Riley's parents got a cell phone plan that has a $40 monthly fee for the first phone. For each extra phone, there is a $15 phone service charge and a $10 text service charge. The expression $40 + 15e + 10e$ represents the total phone bill in dollars, where e is the number of extra phones. Simplify the expression by combining like terms.

_____

3. A radio show lasts for h hours. For every 60 minutes of air time during the show, there are 8 minutes of commercials. The expression $60h - 8h$ represents the air time in minutes available for talk and music. Simplify the expression by combining like terms.

_____

4. A publisher sends 100 books to each bookstore where its books are sold. At each store, about 3 books are sold at a discount to employees and about 40 books are sold during store weekend sales. The expression $100s - 3s - 40s$ represents the approximate number of the publisher's books sold at full price in s stores. Simplify the expression by combining like terms.

_____

5. A sub shop sells a meal that includes an Italian sub for $6 and chips for $2. If a customer purchases more than 3 meals, he or she receives a $5 discount. The expression $6m + 2m - 5$ shows the cost in dollars of the customer's order for m meals, where m is greater than 3. Simplify the expression by combining like terms.

_____

Name _____

Lesson Objective: Use the properties of operations to generate equivalent algebraic expressions.

Generate Equivalent Expressions

Equivalent expressions are two or more expressions that are equal for any value of the variable in the expressions. You can use the properties of operations to write equivalent expressions.

Write an equivalent expression for 4c + 2 + c.

Step 1 Identify like terms. $4c$ and c

Step 2 Use properties of operations to combine like terms.
Commutative Property of Addition: switch 2 and c $4c + 2 + c = 4c + c + 2$
Associative Property of Addition: group $4c$ and c $= (4c + c) + 2$
Add $4c$ and c. $= 5c + 2$

Use properties of operations to write an equivalent expression by combining like terms.

1. $7x + 2x + 5x$ **2.** $8a + 11 - 2a$ **3.** $12b - 8b + 3$

4. $9c - 6 + c$ **5.** $4p + 1 - p$ **6.** $8y - 2y + y$

Use the Distributive Property to write an equivalent expression.

7. $3(m + 7)$ **8.** $4(2t + 3)$

9. $5(9 + 6r)$ **10.** $8(4n - 2n)$

Generate Equivalent Expressions

Use properties of operations to write an equivalent expression by combining like terms.

1. $7h - 3h$

$\underline{\quad 4h \quad}$

2. $5x + 7 + 2x$

3. $16 + 13p - 9p$

4. $y^2 + 13y - 8y$

5. $5(2h + 3) + 3h$

6. $12 + 18n + 7 - 14n$

Use the Distributive Property to write an equivalent expression.

7. $2(9 + 5k)$

8. $5(3m + 2)$

9. $6(g + h)$

10. $4d + 8$

11. $21p + 35q$

12. $18x + 9y$

Problem Solving REAL WORLD

13. The expression $15n + 12n + 100$ represents the total cost in dollars for skis, boots, and a lesson for n skiers. Simplify the expression $15n + 12n + 100$. Then find the total cost for 8 skiers.

14. Casey has n nickels. Megan has 4 times as many nickels as Casey has. Write an expression for the total number of nickels Casey and Megan have. Then simplify the expression.

Identify Equivalent Expressions

Use properties to determine whether $5a + 7(3 + a)$ and $12a + 21$ are equivalent.

Step 1 Rewrite the first expression using the Distributive Property. Multiply 7 and 3 and multiply 7 and a.

$5a + 7(3 + a) = 5a + 21 + 7a$

Step 2 Use the Commutative Property of Addition. Switch 21 and $7a$.

$= 5a + 7a + 21$

Step 3 Use the Associative Property of Addition to group like terms. $5a$ and $7a$ are like terms.

$= (5a + 7a) + 21$

Step 4 Combine like terms.

$= 12a + 21$

Compare the expressions: $12a + 21$ and $12a + 21$. They are the same.
So, the expressions $5a + 7(3 + a)$ and $12a + 21$ are equivalent.

Use properties to determine whether the expressions are equivalent.

1. $6(p + q)$ and $6p + q$

2. $7y - 15 + 2y$ and $9y - 15$

3. $1 + (8r + 9)$ and $(2 + 8) + 8r$

_____

4. $0 \times 11 + 5n$ and $5n$

5. $16s - 4 + s$ and $12s$

6. $11d \times 2$ and $22d$

_____

7. $10(e + 0.5g)$ and $10e + 5g$

8. $8m + (9m - 1)$ and $8m - 8$

9. $7(1 \times 2h)$ and $21h$

_____

Identify Equivalent Expressions

Use properties of operations to determine whether
the expressions are equivalent.

1. $2s + 13 + 15s$ and
$17s + 13$

2. $5 \times 7h$ and $35h$

3. $10 + 8v - 3v$ and $18 - 3v$

__equivalent__
_____   _____   _____

4. $(9w \times 0) - 12$ and $9w - 12$

5. $11(p + q)$ and
$11p + (7q + 4q)$

6. $6(4b + 3d)$ and $24b + 3d$

_____   _____   _____

7. $14m + 9 - 6m$ and $8m + 9$

8. $(y \times 1) + 2$ and $y + 2$

9. $4 + 5(6t + 1)$ and $9 + 30t$

_____   _____   _____

10. $9x + 0 + 10x$ and $19x + 1$

11. $12c - 3c$ and $3(4c - 1)$

12. $6a \times 4$ and $24a$

_____   _____   _____

Problem Solving REAL WORLD

13. Rachel needs to write 3 book reports with
b pages and 3 science reports with s pages
during the school year. Write an algebraic
expression for the total number of pages
Rachel will need to write.

14. Rachel's friend Yassi has to write $3(b + s)$
pages for reports. Use properties of operations
to determine whether this expression is
equivalent to the expression for the number of
pages Rachel has to write.

_____   _____

© Houghton Mifflin Harcourt Publishing Company

Lesson 57
COMMON CORE STANDARD CC.6.EE.5
Lesson Objective: Determine whether a
number is a solution of an equation.

Solutions of Equations

An **equation** is a statement that two mathematical expressions are equal.

Some equations include only numbers, operation signs, and an equal
sign. Example: $2 + 17 = 19$

Other equations also include variables, such as x. Example: $50 - x = 37$

For an equation with a variable, a **solution** is a value of the variable that
makes the equation true.

Equation: $8.6 + m = 13$	Is $m = 5.3$ a solution?	Is $m = 4.4$ a solution?
Step 1 Write the equation.	$8.6 + m = 13$	$8.6 + m = 13$
Step 2 Substitute the given number for the variable m.	$8.6 + 5.3 \overset{?}{=} 13$	$8.6 + 4.4 \overset{?}{=} 13$
Step 3 Add.	$13.9 \neq 13$	$13 = 13$
	($\neq$ means *does not equal*)	
Decide whether the equation is true.	The equation is not true. So, $m = 5.3$ is **not a solution**.	The equation is true. So, $m = 4.4$ is a **solution**.

**Determine whether the given value of the variable is a
solution of the equation.**

1. $p - 4 = 6$; $p = 10$

_____ $- 4 \overset{?}{=} 6$

_____ $\bigcirc$ 6

2. $15.2 + y = 22$; $y = 6.8$

3. $n + 3 = 16$; $n = 12$

4. $7.4 - k = 5$; $k = 3.4$

5. $1\frac{1}{2} + t = 3\frac{1}{2}$; $t = 2$

6. $4x = 36$; $x = 8$

Expressions and Equations

Solutions of Equations

Determine whether the given value of the variable is a solution of the equation.

1. $x - 7 = 15$; $x = 8$

$$\underline{\quad 8 \quad} - 7 \stackrel{?}{=} 15$$

$$\underline{\quad 1 \quad} \enspace \cancel{=} \enspace 15$$

not a solution

2. $c + 11 = 20$; $c = 9$

_____

_____

3. $7n = 7$; $n = 0$

_____

_____

4. $\frac{1}{3}h = 6$; $h = 2$

_____

5. $a - 1 = 70$; $a = 71$

_____

6. $\frac{7}{8} + j = 1$; $j = \frac{1}{8}$

_____

7. $16.1 + d = 22$; $d = 6.1$

_____

8. $9 = \frac{3}{4}e$; $e = 12$

_____

9. $15.5 - y = 7.9$; $y = 8.4$

_____

Problem Solving REAL WORLD

10. Terrance needs to score 25 points to win a game. He has already scored 18 points. The equation $18 + p = 25$ gives the number of points p that Terrance still needs to score. Determine whether $p = 7$ or $p = 13$ is a solution of the equation, and tell what the solution means.

_____

_____

_____

_____

11. Madeline has used 50 sheets of a roll of paper towels, which is $\frac{5}{8}$ of the entire roll. The equation $\frac{5}{8}s = 50$ can be used to find the number of sheets s in a full roll. Determine whether $s = 32$ or $s = 80$ is a solution of the equation, and tell what the solution means.

_____

_____

_____

_____

Solutions of Inequalities

An **inequality** is a mathematical sentence that compares expressions. A **solution of an inequality** is a value for a variable that makes the inequality true.

For the inequality $a < 3$ (a is less than 3), $a = 1$ is a solution because 1 is less than 3. $a = 3$ is *not* a solution because 3 is *not* less than 3.

Inequalities use these symbols: $<$ (less than), $>$ (greater than), $\le$ (less than or equal to), and $\ge$ (greater than or equal to).

	For the inequality $x \le 5$, is $x = 3$ a solution?	For the inequality $y > 8$, is $y = 3$ a solution?
Step 1 Understand the inequality.	$x \le 5$ means "x is less than or equal to 5." Any value that is equal to 5 or less than 5 is a solution.	$y > 8$ means "y is greater than 8." Any value that is greater than 8 is a solution.
Step 2 Decide whether the value is a solution.	3 is less than 5, so $x = 3$ is a solution.	3 is not greater than 8, so $y = 3$ is not a solution.

Determine whether the given value of the variable is a solution of the inequality.

1. $m \ge 4$; $m = 2$

   $m \ge 4$ means "m is

   _____

   _____ 4."

   $m = 2$ is _____

2. $k < 7$; $k = 5$

3. $z \ge 12$; $z = 12$

4. $y \le 3$; $y = 6$

5. $n > 13$; $n = 8$

6. $t < 7$; $t = 5$

Give two solutions of the inequality.

7. $x > 4$

   _____ ; _____

8. $p \le 3$

   _____ ; _____

9. $v \ge 9$

   _____ ; _____

Expressions and Equations

Solutions of Inequalities

Determine whether the given value of the variable is a solution of the inequality.

1. $s \geq {}^-1; s = 1$

$$1 \overset{?}{\geq} {}^-1$$

solution

2. $p < 0; p = 4$

3. $y \leq {}^-3; y = {}^-1$

4. $u > {}^-\frac{1}{2}; u = 0$

5. $q \geq 0.6; q = 0.23$

6. $b < 2\frac{3}{4}; b = \frac{2}{3}$

7. $j \leq {}^-5.7; j = {}^-6$

8. $a > {}^-8; a = {}^-7.5$

9. $w \geq 4.5; w = 4.45$

Give two solutions of the inequality.

10. $k < 2$

11. $z \geq {}^-3$

12. $f \leq {}^-5$

Problem Solving REAL WORLD

13. The inequality $s \geq 92$ represents the score s that Jared must earn on his next test to get an A on his report card. Give two possible scores that Jared could earn to get the A.

14. The inequality $m \leq \$20$ represents the amount of money that Sheila is allowed to spend on a new hat. Give two possible money amounts that Sheila could spend on the hat.

Use Algebraic Expressions

You can use an algebraic expression to help solve a word problem.
Use a variable to represent the unknown number.

Ina wants to serve salad at her party. She will need one head of lettuce for every 6 guests who attend. Write an expression she could use for deciding how much lettuce she needs.

Step 1 Decide what operation the problem uses.	Each head of lettuce will serve 6 people. Divide the number of guests by 6.
Step 2 Identify the unknown number.	The problem does not state how many guests will attend. Use the variable g for the number of guests.
Step 3 Write a word expression. Then use the word expression to write an algebraic expression.	"the number of guests divided by 6" $g \div 6$ or $\dfrac{g}{6}$

Ina finds out that 18 guests will attend. Evaluate the expression for this number of guests.

Step 1 Substitute 18 for g. $\dfrac{18}{6}$ **Step 2** Divide. $\dfrac{18}{6} = 3$

So, Ina will need 3 heads of lettuce.

At her last party, Ina decorated with window stickers. For this party, she wants to use 4 times as many stickers.

1. Write an expression for the number of stickers Ina will use. (Use the variable s to represent the number of stickers she used at her last party.)

   _____

2. Use the expression to find the new number of stickers if she used 14 stickers for her last party.

   _____

3. Ina wants to put an equal number of stickers on each of the windows. Write an expression to show how many stickers will go on each window. (Use the variable w to represent the number of windows.)

   _____

4. Use the expression to find the number of stickers for each window if there are 8 windows.

   _____

Expressions and Equations

Use Algebraic Expressions

Jeff sold the pumpkins he grew for $7 each at the farmer's market.

1. Write an expression to represent the amount of money Jeff made selling the pumpkins. Tell what the variable in your expression represents.

   7p, where p is the number
   of pumpkins

2. If Jeff sold 30 pumpkins, how much money did he make?

An architect is designing a building. Each floor will be 12 feet tall.

3. Write an expression for the number of floors the building can have for a given building height. Tell what the variable in your expression represents.

   _____

   _____

4. If the architect is designing a building that is 132 feet tall, how many floors can be built?

   _____

Write an algebraic expression for each word expression. Then evaluate the expression for these values of the variable: 1, 6, 13.5

5. the quotient of 100 and the sum of b and 24

   _____

   _____

6. 13 more than the product of m and 5

   _____

   _____

Problem Solving REAL WORLD

7. In the town of Pleasant Hill, there is an average of 16 sunny days each month. Write an expression to represent the approximate number of sunny days for any number of months. Tell what the variable represents.

   _____

8. How many sunny days can a resident of Pleasant Hill expect to have in 9 months?

   _____

Lesson 60

COMMON CORE STANDARD CC.6.EE.7
Lesson Objective: Write algebraic equations.

Write Equations

To write an equation for a word sentence, write the words as mathematical expressions and write = for "equals" or "is."

Write an equation for the word sentence.

Example 1 6 fewer than a number is $12\frac{2}{3}$.

Step 1 Choose a variable.
6 fewer than a number is $12\frac{2}{3}$.
Let n represent a number.

Step 2 Identify the operation.

6 fewer than n is $12\frac{2}{3}$.
"Fewer than" means subtract.

Step 3 Write an equation.

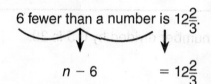

$$n - 6 \qquad = 12\frac{2}{3}$$

So, the equation is $n - 6 = 12\frac{2}{3}$.

Example 2

The quotient of 20.7 gallons and a number is 9 gallons.

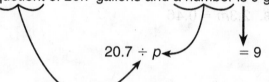

$$20.7 \div p \qquad = 9$$

So, the equation is $20.7 \div p = 9$.

Write an equation for the word sentence.

1. 18 more than a number is 29.

2. 5.2 times a number is 46.8.

3. 128 less than a number is 452.

4. Four fifths of a number equals 11.

5. The product of a number and 6 is 138.

6. The number of miles decreased by 29.8 is 139.

Write Equations

Write an equation for the word sentence.

1. 18 is 4.5 times a number.

$$18 = 4.5n$$

2. Eight more than the number of children is 24.

_____

3. The difference of a number and $\frac{2}{3}$ is $\frac{3}{8}$.

_____

4. m minutes less than 80 minutes is 15 minutes.

_____

5. A number divided by 0.5 is 29.

_____

6. The product of the number of songs and $0.99 is $7.92.

_____

Write a word sentence for the equation.

7. $x - 14 = 52$

_____

8. $2.3m = 0.46$

_____

9. $25 = k \div 5$

_____

10. $4\frac{1}{3} + q = 5\frac{1}{6}$

_____

Problem Solving REAL WORLD

11. An ostrich egg weighs 2.9 pounds. The difference between the weight of this egg and the weight of an emu egg is 1.6 pounds. Write an equation that could be used to find the weight w, in pounds, of the emu egg.

_____

12. In one week, the number of bowls a potter made was 6 times the number of plates. He made 90 bowls during the week. Write an equation that could be used to find the number of plates p that the potter made.

_____

Model and Solve Addition Equations

You can use algebra tiles to model and solve equations. Use a long rectangle to represent the variable, and a square to represent 1.

Model and solve the equation $x + 9 = 11$.

Step 1 Model the equation using algebra tiles.

Step 2 Get the variable by itself on one side of the equation. Remove the same number of tiles from each side.

Step 3 Write the solution.

$x = 2$

Solve the equation by using algebra tiles or by drawing a picture.

1. $x + 4 = 10$

2. $8 = x + 2$

Expressions and Equations

Model and Solve Addition Equations

Model and solve the equation by using algebra tiles.

1. $x + 6 = 9$ **2.** $x + 5 = 6$ **3.** $9 = x + 1$

$$x = 3$$

_____ _____

4. $8 + x = 10$ **5.** $x + 7 = 11$ **6.** $4 = 2 + x$

_____ _____ _____

Solve the equation by drawing a model.

7. $x + 4 = 7$ **8.** $x + 6 = 10$

_____ _____

Problem Solving

9. The temperature at 10:00 was 10°F. This is 3°F warmer than the temperature at 8:00. Model and solve the equation $x + 3 = 10$ to find the temperature x in degrees Fahrenheit at 8:00.

10. Jaspar has 7 more checkers left than Karen does. Jaspar has 9 checkers left. Write and solve an addition equation to find out how many checkers Karen has left.

_____ _____

Lesson 62
COMMON CORE STANDARD CC.6.EE.7
Lesson Objective: Use algebra to solve
addition and subtraction equations.

Solve Addition and Subtraction Equations

To solve an equation, you must isolate the variable on one side of the equal sign. You can use **inverse operations**: undoing addition with subtraction or subtraction with addition. These actions are made possible by the **Addition and Subtraction Properties of Equality.**

Solve and check.

Example 1: $y + 6.7 = 9.8$ **Example 2:** $57 = x - 8$

Step 1 Look at the side with the variable. Subtract the number that is added to the variable, or add the number that is subtracted from the variable. Be sure to perform the <u>same</u> operation on <u>both</u> sides of the equation.

$y + 6.7 = 9.8$ $57 = x - 8$

$y + 6.7 - 6.7 = 9.8 - 6.7$ Subtract 6.7 from $57 + 8 = x - 8 + 8$ Add 8 to
                               both sides.   both sides.

Step 2 Simplify both sides of the equation.

$y + 6.7 = 9.8$ $57 = x - 8$

$y + 6.7 - 6.7 = 9.8 - 6.7$ $57 + 8 = x - 8 + 8$

$y + 0 = 3.1$ $65 = x + 0$

$y = 3.1$ $65 = x$

Step 3 Check your answer in the original equation.

$y + 6.7 = 9.8$ $57 = x - 8$

$3.1 + 6.7 \overset{?}{=} 9.8$ $57 \overset{?}{=} 65 - 8$

$9.8 = 9.8$ $57 = 57$

So, $y = 3.1$ is the solution.   So, $x = 65$ is the solution.

Solve and check.

1. $x + 13 = 27$ **2.** $38 = d - 22$ **3.** $12.4 = a + 7.9$ **4.** $w - 2\frac{3}{5} = 4\frac{2}{5}$

Solve Addition and Subtraction Equations

Solve the equation, and check the solution.

1. $y - 14 = 23$

$$y - 14 + 14 = 23 + 14$$
$$y = 37$$

2. $x + 3 = 15$

3. $n + \frac{2}{5} = \frac{4}{5}$

4. $16 = m - 14$

5. $w - 13.7 = 22.8$

6. $s + 55 = 55$

7. $23 = x - 12$

8. $p - 14 = 14$

9. $m - 2\frac{3}{4} = 6\frac{1}{2}$

10. $t + 0.95 = 1.25$

11. $3\frac{1}{3} = b - \frac{2}{3}$

12. $48 = d + 23$

Problem Solving REAL WORLD

13. A recipe calls for $5\frac{1}{2}$ cups of flour. Lorenzo only has $3\frac{3}{4}$ cups of flour. Write and solve an equation to find the additional amount of flour Lorenzo needs to make the recipe.

14. Jan used 22.5 gallons of water in the shower. This amount is 7.5 gallons less than the amount she used for washing clothes. Write and solve an equation to find the amount of water Jan used to wash clothes.

Model and Solve Multiplication Equations

You can use algebra tiles or a drawing to model and solve equations. Use a rectangle to represent the variable and a square to represent 1.

Model and solve the equation 3x = 9.

Step 1 Model the equation using rectangles and squares.

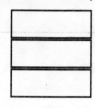 =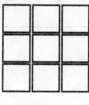

3x   =   9

Step 2 Divide the squares into equal groups. The number of groups should be the same as the number of rectangles.

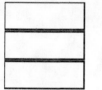

3x   =   9

Step 3 Find the number of squares in each group.

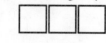

x   =   3

So, x = 3 is the solution.

Solve the equation by using algebra tiles or by drawing a picture.

1. 4x = 12

2. 2x = 16

Expressions and Equations

Model and Solve Multiplication Equations

Model and solve the equation by using algebra tiles.

1. $2x = 8$

2. $5x = 10$

3. $21 = 3x$

$$\underline{\hspace{3em} x = 4 \hspace{3em}}$$

4. $4x = 20$

5. $6x = 6$

6. $4 = 2x$

Solve the equation by drawing a model.

7. $6 = 3x$

8. $4x = 12$

Problem Solving

9. A chef used 20 eggs to make 5 omelets. Model and solve the equation $5x = 20$ to find the number of eggs x in each omelet.

10. Last month, Julio played 3 times as many video games as Scott did. Julio played 18 video games. Write and solve an equation to find the number of video games Scott played.

© Houghton Mifflin Harcourt Publishing Company

COMMON CORE STANDARD CC.6.EE.7
Lesson Objective: Use algebra to solve
multiplication and division equations.

Solve Multiplication and Division Equations

A multiplication equation shows a variable multiplied by a number.
A division equation shows a variable divided by a number. To solve a
multiplication equation, you use the **Division Property of Equality**.
To solve a division equation, you use the **Multiplication Property of
Equality**. These properties state that both sides of an equation remain
equal when you multiply or divide both sides by the same number.

Solve and check.

Example 1: $\frac{a}{5} = 6$ **Example 2:** $2.5x = 10$

Step 1 Look at the side with the variable. Use the inverse operation to get the variable by itself.

$\frac{a}{5} = 6$	a is divided by 5.	$2.5x = 10$	x is multiplied by 2.5.
$5 \times \frac{a}{5} = 6 \times 5$	Multiply both sides by 5.	$\frac{2.5x}{2.5} = \frac{10}{2.5}$	Divide both sides by 2.5.

Step 2 Simplify both sides of the equation.

$$\frac{a}{5} = 6 \qquad\qquad\qquad 2.5x = 10$$

$$5 \times \frac{a}{5} = 6 \times 5 \qquad\qquad \frac{2.5x}{2.5} = \frac{10}{2.5}$$

$$a = 30 \qquad\qquad\qquad x = 4$$

Step 3 Check your answer in the original equation.

$$\frac{a}{5} = 6 \qquad\qquad\qquad 2.5x = 10$$

$$\frac{30}{5} \stackrel{?}{=} 6 \qquad\qquad\qquad 2.5 \times 4 \stackrel{?}{=} 10$$

$$6 = 6 \qquad\qquad\qquad 10 = 10$$

So, $a = 30$ is the solution.   So, $x = 4$ is the solution.

Solve and check.

1. $3x = 42$ **2.** $4c = 48$ **3.** $12.8 = 3.2d$ **4.** $12 = 1.5w$

_____   _____   _____   _____

5. $\frac{z}{6} = 9$ **6.** $\frac{d}{4} = 5$ **7.** $11 = \frac{n}{2.4}$ **8.** $12 = \frac{4}{5}k$

_____   _____   _____   _____

Solve Multiplication and Division Equations

Solve the equation, and check the solution.

1. $8p = 96$

$$\frac{8p}{8} = \frac{96}{8}$$
$$p = 12$$

2. $\frac{z}{16} = 8$

3. $3.5x = 14.7$

4. $32 = 3.2c$

5. $\frac{2}{5}w = 40$

6. $\frac{a}{14} = 6.8$

7. $1.6x = 1.6$

8. $23.8 = 3.5b$

9. $\frac{3}{5} = \frac{2}{3}t$

10. $\frac{x}{7} = 0$

11. $4n = 9$

12. $\frac{3}{4}g = \frac{5}{8}$

Problem Solving REAL WORLD

13. Anne runs 6 laps on a track. She runs a total of 1 mile, or 5,280 feet. Write and solve an equation to find the distance, in feet, that she runs in each lap.

14. DeShawn uses $\frac{3}{4}$ of a box of rice to cook dinner. The portion he uses weighs 12 ounces. Write and solve an equation to find the weight of the full box of rice.

Lesson 65

COMMON CORE STANDARD CC.6.EE.7
Lesson Objective: Solve equations involving fractions by using the strategy *solve a simpler problem.*

Problem Solving • Equations with Fractions

After driving 25 miles, Kevin has traveled $\frac{2}{3}$ of the distance from his house to his friend's house. Use the equation $25 = \frac{2}{3}d$ to find the total distance d in miles to his friend's house.

Read the Problem

What do I need to find?	What information do I need to use?	How will I use the information?
I need to find the _____ _____ from Kevin's house to _____ _____.	I need to use the equation _____.	I can use multiplication to change the equation to an equation with only _____, not fractions. Then I can _____ the new equation.

Solve the Problem

Step 1 Write the original equation. $25 = \frac{2}{3}d$

Step 2 Write a simpler equation without fractions. Multiply both $3 \times 25 = (3 \times \frac{2}{3})d$
sides by the denominator of the fraction. $75 = \frac{6}{3}d$

$75 = 2d$

Step 3 Solve the simpler equation. Use the Division Property of Equality. $\frac{75}{2} = \frac{2d}{2}$

$37.5 = d$

So, the total distance is 37.5 miles.

Solve.

1. Alyssa's cat weighs 12 pounds, which is $\frac{3}{8}$ of the weight of her dog. Use the equation $\frac{3}{8}d = 12$ to find the weight of Alyssa's dog.

_____

2. Randall bought 16 baseball cards from Max, which is $\frac{2}{5}$ of Max's collection. Use the equation $16 = \frac{2}{5}c$ to find the number of cards that were in Max's collection.

_____

Name _____

Lesson 65

CC.6.EE.7segment>

Problem Solving • Equations with Fractions

Read each problem and solve.

1. Stu is 4 feet tall. This height represents $\frac{6}{7}$ of his brother's height. The equation $\frac{6}{7}h = 4$ can be used to find the height h, in feet, of Stu's brother. How tall is Stu's brother?

$$7 \times \frac{6}{7}h = 7 \times 4$$
$$6h = 28$$
$$\frac{6h}{6} = \frac{28}{6}$$
$$h = 4\frac{2}{3}$$
$$4\frac{2}{3} \text{ feet}$$

2. Bryce bought a bag of cashews. He served $\frac{7}{8}$ pound of cashews at a party. This amount represents $\frac{2}{3}$ of the entire bag. The equation $\frac{2}{3}n = \frac{7}{8}$ can be used to find the number of pounds n in a full bag. How many pounds of cashews were in the bag that Bryce bought?

_____

3. In Jaime's math class, 9 students chose soccer as their favorite sport. This amount represents $\frac{3}{8}$ of the entire class. The equation $\frac{3}{8}s = 9$ can be used to find the total number of students s in Jaime's class. How many students are in Jaime's math class?

_____

4. There are 15 blueberry muffins in a large basket. This represents $\frac{5}{9}$ of all the muffins that are in the basket. The equation $\frac{5}{9}m = 15$ can be used to find the total number of muffins m in the basket. How many muffins are in the basket?

_____

Name _____

Lesson 66

COMMON CORE STANDARD CC.6.EE.8
Lesson Objective: Write algebraic inequalities.

Write Inequalities

Here are some ways to express each inequality symbol in words:

<	less than	under	not as much as
≤	less than or equal to	at most	no more than

>	greater than	over	more than
≥	greater than or equal to	at least	no less than

Passengers at least 12 years old pay full price for train tickets.
Write an inequality to represent the situation.

Step 1 Choose a variable. Use a to represent "age." a

Step 2 Choose an inequality symbol. "at least 12 years old"
means "greater than or equal to 12." $\geq$

Step 3 Write the inequality. $a \geq 12$

Write two word sentences to represent $y < 9$.

Step 1 Identify the inequality symbol. $<$ means "less than."

Step 2 Write a word sentence that uses the variable and integer. y is less than 9.

Step 3 Write another word sentence with the same meaning. y is under 9.

Write an inequality for the word sentence.

1. The distance d Mr. Chin drove was no more than 65 miles.

_____

2. The amount of juice c in the punch is more than 3 cups.

_____

3. The age a of Mia's sister is less than 8 years.

_____

4. The temperature t was at least 30°F.

_____

Write two word sentences to represent the inequality.

5. $n \geq 23$

_____

_____

6. $p > 16$

_____

_____

Expressions and Equations

Write Inequalities

Write an inequality for the word sentence. Tell what type of numbers the variable in the inequality can represent.

1. The width w is greater than 4 centimeters.

   The inequality symbol for "is greater than" is $>$.
   $w > 4$, where w is the width in centimeters. w is
   a positive number.

2. The score s in a basketball game is greater than or equal to 10 points.

3. The mass m is less than 5 kilograms.

4. The height h is greater than 2.5 meters.

5. The temperature t is less than or equal to $^{-}3°$.

Write a word sentence for the inequality.

6. $k < ^{-}7$

7. $z \geq 14$

8. $m \leq 2\frac{3}{5}$

9. $f > 0.24$

Problem Solving REAL WORLD

10. Tabby's mom says that she must read for at least 30 minutes each night. If m represents the number of minutes reading, what inequality can represent this situation?

11. Phillip has a $25 gift card to his favorite restaurant. He wants to use the gift card to buy lunch. If c represents the cost of his lunch, what inequality can describe all of the possible amounts of money, in dollars, that Phillip can spend on lunch?

Lesson 67

COMMON CORE STANDARD CC.6.EE.8

Lesson Objective: Represent solutions of algebraic inequalities on number line diagrams.

Graph Inequalities

You can graph the solutions of an inequality on a number line.

Graph the inequality $n \geq 9$.

Step 1 Determine the meaning of the inequality.
$n \geq 9$ means "n is greater than or equal to 9."

Step 2 Draw a number line and circle the number given in the inequality.

Step 3 Decide whether to fill in the circle.
For $\leq$ or $\geq$, fill in the circle to show "or equal to." For $<$ or $>$, do not fill in the circle.

Since the inequality uses $\geq$, 9 is a possible solution. So, fill in the circle.

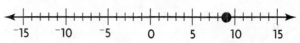

Step 4 Shade from the circle in the direction of the remaining solutions.

Since the inequality symbol is $\geq$, the shading covers all numbers greater than 9.

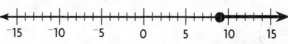

Graph the inequality.

1. $k < 8$

2. $r \geq 6$

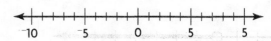

3. $w \leq 3$

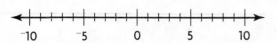

4. $x > 3$

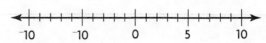

Write the inequality shown by the graph.

5.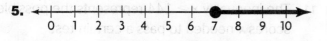

0 1 2 3 4 5 6 7 8 9 10

_____

6.

0 1 2 3 4 5 6 7 8 9 10

_____

Name _____

Lesson 67

CC.6.EE.8

Graph Inequalities

Graph the inequality.

1. $h \geq 3$

   Draw a filled-in circle at __3__ to show that 3 is a solution. Shade to the **right** of __3__ to show that values greater than 3 are solutions.

2. $x < -\dfrac{4}{5}$

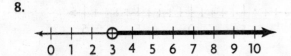

3. $y > {}^{-}2$

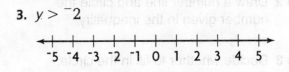

4. $b < 8$

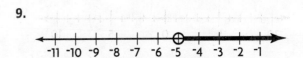

5. $m \leq 3$

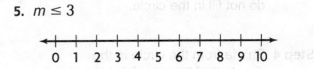

6. $n \geq 1\dfrac{1}{2}$

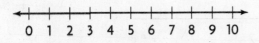

7. $c \leq {}^{-}0.4$

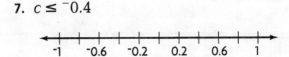

Write the inequality represented by the graph.

8.

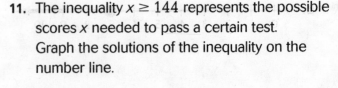

_____

9.

_____

Problem Solving REAL WORLD

10. The inequality $x \leq 2$ represents the elevation x of a certain object found at a dig site. Graph the solutions of the inequality on the number line.

11. The inequality $x \geq 144$ represents the possible scores x needed to pass a certain test. Graph the solutions of the inequality on the number line.

Lesson 68

COMMON CORE STANDARD CC.6.EE.9

Lesson Objective: Write an equation to represent the relationship between an independent variable and a dependent variable.

Independent and Dependent Variables

An equation with two variables shows a relationship between two quantities. The value of the **dependent variable** changes according to the value of the **independent variable.**

Sam rides the bus almost every day. He pays $2.50 for each bus ride.

Identify the dependent and independent variables in this situation. Then write an equation to represent the relationship between the total cost and the number of bus rides.

Step 1 Understand the relationship and identify variables.

Each bus ride costs $2.50. The total cost c for Sam's bus rides depends on the number of rides r he takes. The value of c will change when the value of r changes.

So, c is the dependent variable and r is the independent variable.

Step 2 Write an equation. The total cost will be $2.50 multiplied by the number of rides.

$c = 2.50 \times r$
(or $c = 2.50r$)

Use your equation to find out how much it would cost for Sam to take 4 bus rides.

Step 1 Think: 4 bus rides means $r = 4$.

Step 2 Substitute 4 for r in the equation.

$c = 2.50 \times r$
$c = 2.50 \times 4$
$c = 10.00$

So, Sam's total cost will be $10.00 for 4 rides.

Identify the dependent and independent variables. Write an equation to show the relationship between them. Then solve for the given value.

1. Janna is buying a netbook with a flash drive. The total cost c will include the price p of the netbook, plus $12.50 for the flash drive.

Find the total cost if the price of the netbook is $375.00.

The _____ depends on the

_____.

dependent variable: _____ independent variable: _____

equation: _____ = _____ + _____

Total cost: c = _____ + _____

c = _____

Independent and Dependent Variables

Identify the independent and dependent variables. Then write an equation to represent the relationship between them.

1. Sandra has a coupon to save $3 off her next purchase at a restaurant. The cost of her meal c will be the price of the food p that she orders, minus $3.

The ___cost of her meal___ depends on the ___price of her food___.

dependent variable: ___c___

independent variable: ___p___

equation: ___c___ = ___$p - 3$___

2. An online clothing store charges $6 for shipping, no matter the price of the items. The total cost c in dollars is the price of the items ordered p plus $6 for shipping.

dependent variable: _____

independent variable: _____

equation: _____ = _____

3. Melinda is making necklaces. She uses 12 beads for each necklace. The total number of beads b depends on the number of necklaces n.

dependent variable: _____

independent variable: _____

equation: _____ = _____

4. Tanner is 2 years younger than his brother. Tanner's age t in years is 2 less than his brother's age b.

dependent variable: _____

independent variable: _____

equation: _____ = _____

5. Byron is playing a game. He earns 10 points for each question he answers correctly. His total score s equals the number of correct answers a times 10.

dependent variable: _____

independent variable: _____

equation: _____ = _____

Problem Solving REAL WORLD

6. Maria earns $45 for every lawn that she mows. Her earnings e in dollars depend on the number of lawns n that she mows. Write an equation that represents this situation.

_____

7. Martin sells cars. He earns $100 per day, plus any commission on his sales. His daily salary s in dollars depends on the amount of commission c. Write an equation to represent his daily salary.

_____

Equations and Tables

You can use tables and equations to represent the relationship between two quantities.

Use the equation to complete the table.

$y = x \div 4$

Step 1 Look at the equation to find the rule. The rule for finding y is $x \div 4$.

Step 2 Apply the rule and fill in the missing values. Divide each x-value by 4.

$44 \div 4 = 11$ $36 \div 4 = 9$ $28 \div 4 = 7$ $20 \div 4 = 5$

x	y
44	
36	
28	
20	

Write an equation for the relationship.

Input, x	30	35	40	45	50
Output, y	6	7	8	9	10

Find a pattern.
Think: "What can I do to each x-value to find its corresponding y-value?"
The y-values are less than the x-values, so try dividing or subtracting.

$30 \div 5 = 6$ $35 \div 5 = 7$ $40 \div 5 = 8$ $45 \div 5 = 9$ $50 \div 5 = 10$

The pattern is to divide x by 5 to get y. The equation is $y = x \div 5$.

Write an equation for the relationship shown in the table.
Then find the missing value in the table.

1.

x	20	40	60	80
y	23	43		83

_____

2.

x	3	4	5	6
y	18	24	30	

Use the equation to complete the table.

3. $y = 7x$

Input, x	1	2	3	4
Output, y	7			

4. $y = x - 2$

Input, x	5	8	11	14
Output, y				

Equations and Tables

Use the equation to complete the table.

1. $y = 6x$

Input	Output
x	y
2	**12**
5	**30**
8	**48**

2. $y = x - 7$

Input	Output
x	y
10	
15	
20	

3. $y = 3x + 4$

Input	Output
x	y
3	
4	
5	

Write an equation for the relationship shown in the table. Then find the unknown value in the table.

4.

x	2	3	4	5
y	16	?	32	40

5.

x	18	20	22	24
y	9	10	?	12

_____

_____

6.

x	8	10	12	14
y	13	15	17	?

7.

x	14	17	20	23
y	5	?	11	14

_____

_____

Problem Solving

8. Tickets to a play cost $11 each. There is also a service charge of $4 per order. Write an equation for the relationship that gives the total cost y in dollars for an order of x tickets.

_____

9. Write an equation for the relationship shown in the table. Then use the equation to find the estimated number of shrimp in a 5-pound bag.

Weight of bag (pounds), x	1	2	3	4
Estimated number of shrimp, y	24	48	72	96

_____

Problem Solving • Analyze Relationships

The table shows the number of miles an overnight train travels. If the pattern in the table continues, how far will the train travel in 10 hours?

Overnight Train Travel Rate				
Time (hours)	1	2	3	4
Distance (miles)	60	120	180	240

Use the graphic organizer to help you solve the problem.

Read the Problem		
What do I need to find?	**What information do I need to use?**	**How will I use the information?**
I need to find the _____ the train will travel in _____ hours.	I need to find the relationship between _____ and _____ shown in the table.	I will find a _____ in the table and use the pattern to write an _____.

Solve the Problem

Look for a pattern between the number of hours and the number of miles.

Overnight Train Travel Rate				
Time in hours, h	1	2	3	4
Distance in miles, m	60	120	180	240

$1 \times 60 \quad 2 \times$ ___ ___ $\times$ ___ ___ $\times$ ___

Then write an equation to show the pattern.

Equation: $m =$ ___ $\times h$

To find the miles the train will travel in 10 hours, substitute 10 for h.

$m =$ ___ $\times$ ___

$m =$ ___

1. The table shows how much a restaurant pays for coffee. How much will the restaurant pay for 100 pounds of coffee?

Coffee Purchasing				
Pounds, p	5	10	30	60
Cost, c	$20	$40	$120	$240

_____

Problem Solving • Analyze Relationships

The table shows the number of cups of yogurt needed to make different amounts of a fruit smoothie. Use the table for 1–3.

Batches, b	3	4	5	6
Cups of Yogurt, c	9	12	15	18

1. Write an equation to represent the relationship.

   The number of cups needed is ___**3**___ multiplied by the number of batches,

   so ___c___ = ___**3**___ × ___b___ .

2. How much yogurt is needed for 9 batches of smoothie? _____

3. Jerry used 33 cups of yogurt to make smoothies. How many batches did he make? _____

The table shows the relationship between Winn's age and his sister's age. Use the table for 4–6.

Winn's age, w	8	9	10	11
Winn's sister's age, s	12	13	14	15

4. Write an equation to represent the relationship. $s =$ _____

5. When Winn is 14 years old, how old will his sister be? _____

6. When Winn's sister is 23 years old, how old will Winn be? _____

Graph Relationships

You can use a graph to represent a relationship.

Graph the relationship represented by the table to find the unknown value of _y_.

x	1	3	5	7
y	4	6	▢	10

Step 1 Write ordered pairs that you know.

(1, 4), (3, 6), (7, 10)

Step 2 Plot the points.

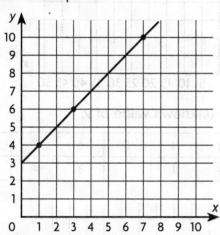

Step 3 Find the unknown _y_-value. Use a ruler to draw a line through the points.
Find the _y_-value that corresponds to an _x_-value of 5.

So, when the _x_-value is 5, the _y_-value is 8.

Graph the relationship represented by the table to find the unknown value of _y_.

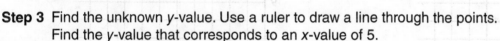

1.

x	1	2	3	4	5
y	3	4	▢	6	7

2.

x	2	4	6	8	10
y	8	7	▢	5	4

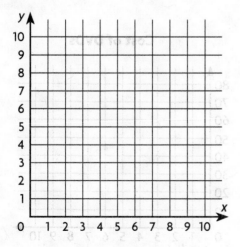

_____

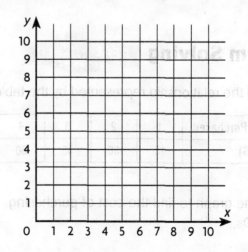

_____

Expressions and Equations

Graph Relationships

Graph the relationship represented by the table.

1.

x	1	2	3	4	5
y	25	50	75	100	125

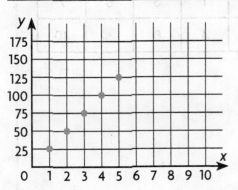

2.

x	10	20	30	40	50
y	350	300	250	200	150

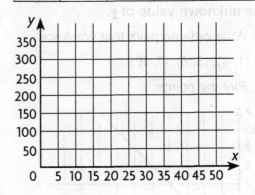

Graph the relationship represented by the table to find the unknown value of y.

3.

x	3	4	5	6	7
y	8	7		5	4

4.

x	1	3	5	7	9
y	1		3	4	5

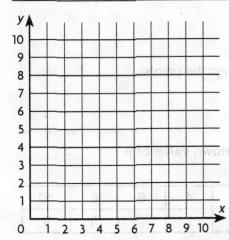

Problem Solving REAL WORLD

5. Graph the relationship represented by the table.

DVDs Purchased	1	2	3	4
Cost ($)	15	30	45	60

6. Use the graph to find the cost of purchasing 5 DVDs.

_____

Cost of DVDs

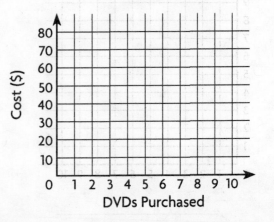

Name _____

Equations and Graphs

You can make a table of values for any equation. Use the table to write ordered pairs. Plot points to help you graph the equation. The graph of a **linear equation** is a straight line.

Graph the linear equation.

$y = x + 1$ $y = 3x - 2$

Step 1 Find ordered pairs that are solutions of the equation.

Choose four values for x. Substitute each value for x in the equation and find the corresponding value of y. Use easy values for x, such as 1, 2, 3, 4.

x	x + 1	y	Ordered Pair
1	1 + 1	2	(1, 2)
2	2 + 1	3	(2, 3)
3	3 + 1	4	(3, 4)
4	4 + 1	5	(4, 5)

x	3x − 2	y	Ordered Pair
1	3 · 1 − 2	1	(1, 1)
2	3 · 2 − 2	4	(2, 4)
3	3 · 3 − 2	7	(3, 7)
4	3 · 4 − 2	10	(4, 10)

Step 2 Graph the equation.

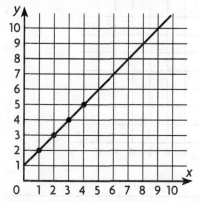   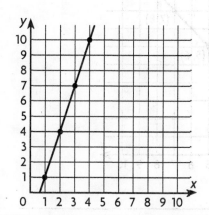

Graph the linear equation.

1. $y = x - 1$

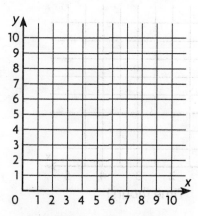

2. $y = 2x - 1$

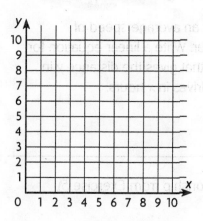

Expressions and Equations

143

Equations and Graphs

Graph the linear equation.

1. $y = x - 3$

x	y
5	2
6	3
7	4
8	5

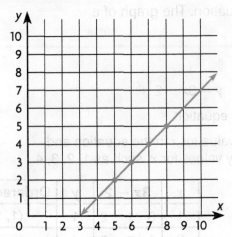

2. $y = x \div 3$

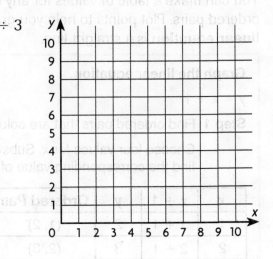

Write a linear equation for the relationship shown by the graph.

3.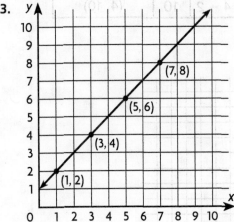

4.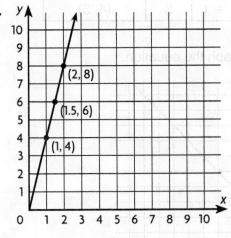

Problem Solving

5. Dee is driving at an average speed of 50 miles per hour. Write a linear equation for the relationship that gives the distance y in miles that Dee drives in x hours.

_____

6. Graph the relationship from Exercise 5.

Dee's Distance

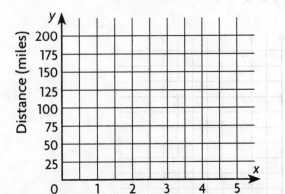

Algebra • Area of Parallelograms

The formula for the area of a parallelogram is the product of the base and height.

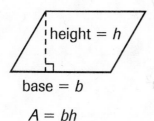

$$A = bh$$

The formula for the area of a square is the square of one of its sides.

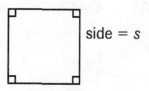

$$A = s^2$$

Find the area.

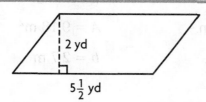

Step 1 Identify the figure.

The figure is a parallelogram, so use the formula $A = bh$.

Step 2 Substitute $5\frac{1}{2}$ for b and 2 for h.

$A = 5\frac{1}{2} \times 2$

Step 3 Multiply.

$A = 5\frac{1}{2} \times 2 = \frac{11}{2} \times \frac{2}{1} = 11$

So, the area of the parallelogram is 11 yd².

Find the area.

1.

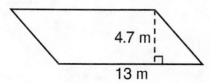

Figure: _____

Formula: $A = $ _____

$A = $ _____ $\times$ _____ $=$ _____ m²

2.

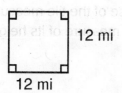

3.

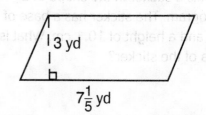

_____ mi²

_____ yd²

Geometry

Area of Parallelograms

Find the area of the figure.

1.
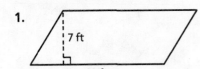

7 ft

18 ft

$A = bh$
$A = 18 \times 7$
$A = 126 \ ft^2$

2.
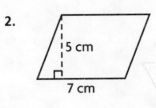

5 cm

7 cm

_____ cm²

Find the unknown measurement for the figure.

3. square

$A =$ _____

$s = 9$ yd

4. parallelogram

$A = 247 \ in.^2$

$b = 19$ in.

$h =$ _____

5. parallelogram

$A = 9.18 \ m^2$

$b = 2.7$ m

$h =$ _____

6. parallelogram

$A = 8\frac{3}{4} \ yd^2$

$b = 3\frac{1}{2}$ yd

$h =$ _____

7. parallelogram

$A = 0.2 \ in.^2$

$b =$ _____

$h = 0.4$ in.

8. parallelogram

$A =$ _____

$b = 4\frac{3}{10}$ m

$h = 2\frac{1}{10}$ m

9. square

$A =$ _____

$s = 35$ cm

10. parallelogram

$A = 6.3 \ mm^2$

$b =$ _____

$h = 0.9$ mm

Problem Solving REAL WORLD

11. Ronna has a sticker in the shape of a parallelogram. The sticker has a base of 6.5 cm and a height of 10.1 cm. What is the area of the sticker?

12. A parallelogram-shaped tile has an area of 48 in.². The base of the tile measures 12 in. What is the measure of its height?

_____

_____

Explore Area of Triangles

You can use grid paper to find a relationship between the areas of triangles and rectangles.

Step 1 On grid paper, draw a rectangle with a base of 8 units and a height of 6 units. Find and record the area of the rectangle.

$A =$ __**48 square units**__

Step 2 Cut out the rectangle.

Step 3 Draw a diagonal from the bottom left corner up to the top right corner.

Step 4 Cut the rectangle along the diagonal.

You have made 2 __**triangles**__.

• Are the triangles congruent? __**yes**__

• How does the area of one triangle compare to the area of the rectangle?

The area of the triangle is half the area of the rectangle.

If *l* is the length and *w* is the width, you can use a rectangle to find the area of a triangle.

Find the area of the triangle.

Area of rectangle: $A = lw = 7 \times 4 = 28 \text{ m}^2$

Area of triangle: $A = \frac{1}{2} \times$ area of rectangle $= \frac{1}{2} \times 28 = 14 \text{ m}^2$

So, the area is __**14**__ square meters.

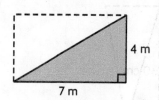

4 m

7 m

Find the area of the triangle.

1.

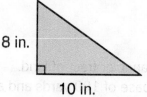

8 in.

10 in.

_____

2.

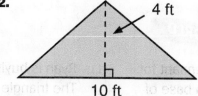

4 ft

10 ft

_____

3.

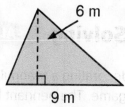

6 m

9 m

_____

Name _____

Lesson 74

CC.6.G.1

Explore Area of Triangles

Find the area of each triangle.

1.

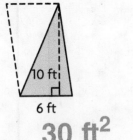

10 ft
6 ft

30 ft²
_____

2.

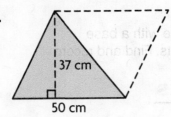

37 cm
50 cm

_____

3.

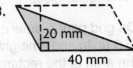

20 mm
40 mm

_____

4.

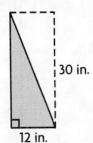

30 in.
12 in.

_____

5.

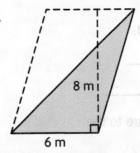

8 m
6 m

_____

6.

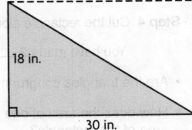

18 in.
30 in.

_____

7.

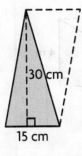

30 cm
15 cm

_____

8.

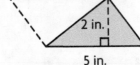

2 in.
5 in.

_____

9.

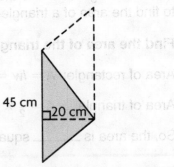

45 cm
20 cm

_____

Problem Solving REAL WORLD

10. Fabian is decorating a triangular pennant for a football game. The pennant has a base of 10 inches and a height of 24 inches. What is the total area of the pennant?

_____

11. Ryan is buying a triangular tract of land. The triangle has a base of 100 yards and a height of 300 yards. What is the area of the tract of land?

_____

148

© Houghton Mifflin Harcourt Publishing Company

Algebra • Area of Triangles

To find the area of a triangle, use the formula
$A = \frac{1}{2} \times$ base $\times$ height.

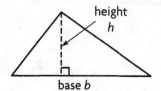

height
h

base b

Find the area of the triangle.

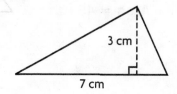

3 cm

7 cm

Step 1 Write the formula.

$A = \frac{1}{2} bh$

Step 2 Rewrite the formula.
Substitute the base and height measurements for b and h.

$A = \frac{1}{2} \times 7 \times 3$

Step 3 Simplify by multiplying.

$A = \frac{1}{2} \times 21$

$A = 10.5$

Step 4 Use the appropriate units.

$A = 10.5 \text{ cm}^2$

Find the area of the triangle.

1.

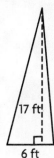

17 ft

6 ft

Write the formula.

$A = \frac{1}{2} \times$ _____

Substitute for b and h.

$A = \frac{1}{2} \times$ _____ $\times$ _____

Simplify.

$A = \frac{1}{2} \times$ _____

$A =$ _____ ft^2

2.

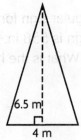

6.5 m

4 m

$A =$ _____

3.

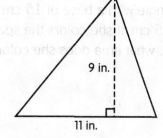

9 in.

11 in.

$A =$ _____

Name _____

Lesson 75
CC.6.G.1

Area of Triangles

Find the area.

1.

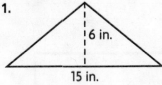

6 in.

15 in.

$A = \frac{1}{2}bh$

$A = \frac{1}{2} \times 15 \times 6$

$A = 45$

Area = 45 in.^{2}

2.

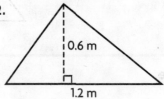

0.6 m

1.2 m

_____

3.

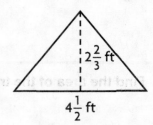

$2\frac{2}{3}$ ft

$4\frac{1}{2}$ ft

_____

Find the unknown measurement for the triangle.

4. $A = 0.225$ mi^2

$b = 0.6$ mi

$h =$

_____

5. $A = 4.86$ yd^2

$b =$

$h = 1.8$ yd

_____

6. $A = 63$ m^2

$b =$

$h = 12$ m

_____

7. $A = 2.5$ km^2

$b = 5$ km

$h =$

_____

Problem Solving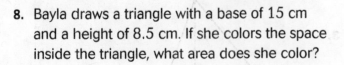

8. Bayla draws a triangle with a base of 15 cm and a height of 8.5 cm. If she colors the space inside the triangle, what area does she color?

_____

9. Alicia is making a triangular sign for the school play. The area of the sign is 558 in.^{2}. The base of the triangle is 36 in. What is the height of the triangle?

_____

150

© Houghton Mifflin Harcourt Publishing Company

Lesson 76

COMMON CORE STANDARD CC.6.G.1

Lesson Objective: Investigate the relationship between the areas of trapezoids and parallelograms.

Explore Area of Trapezoids

Show the relationship between the areas of trapezoids and parallelograms.

Step 1 On grid paper, draw two copies of the trapezoid. Count the grid squares to make your trapezoid match this one.

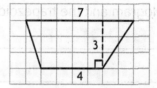

Step 2 Cut out the trapezoids.

Step 3 Turn one trapezoid until the two trapezoids form a parallelogram.

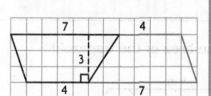

Step 4 Find the length of the base of the parallelogram. Add the lengths of one shorter trapezoid base and one longer trapezoid base.

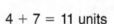
4 + 7 = 11 units

Step 5 Find the area of the parallelogram. Use the formula $A = bh$.

$A = 11 \times 3 = 33$ square units

Step 6 The parallelogram is made of two congruent trapezoids. So, divide by 2 to find the area of one trapezoid.

$33 \div 2 = 16.5$ square units

Find the area of the trapezoid.

1. Trace and cut out two copies of the trapezoid. Arrange them to form a parallelogram.

   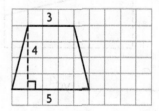

   a. Find the base of the parallelogram. 3 + _____ = _____

   b. Find the area of the parallelogram, using $A = bh$.

   $A =$ _____ × _____ = _____ square units

   c. Find the area of the trapezoid.

   _____ ÷ 2 = _____ square units

2.
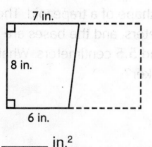
_____ in.²

3.
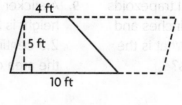
_____ ft²

4.
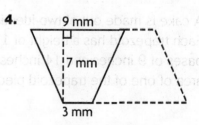
_____ mm²

Explore Area of Trapezoids

1. Trace and cut out two copies of the trapezoid. Arrange the trapezoids to form a parallelogram. Find the areas of the parallelogram and the trapezoids using square units.

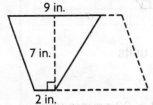

parallelogram: 24 square units; trapezoids: 12 square units

Find the area of the trapezoid.

2.
   9 in.
   7 in.
   2 in.

   _____ in.²

3.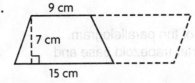
   9 cm
   7 cm
   15 cm

   _____ cm²

4.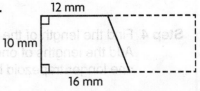
   12 mm
   10 mm
   16 mm

   _____ mm²

5.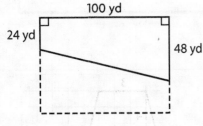
   100 yd
   24 yd
   48 yd

   _____ yd²

6.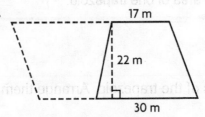
   17 m
   22 m
   30 m

   _____ m²

7.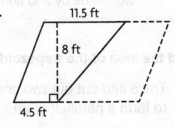
   11.5 ft
   8 ft
   4.5 ft

   _____ ft²

Problem Solving

8. A cake is made out of two identical trapezoids. Each trapezoid has a height of 11 inches and bases of 9 inches and 14 inches. What is the area of one of the trapezoid pieces?

   _____

9. A sticker is in the shape of a trapezoid. The height is 3 centimeters, and the bases are 2.5 centimeters and 5.5 centimeters. What is the area of the sticker?

   _____

Algebra • Area of Trapezoids

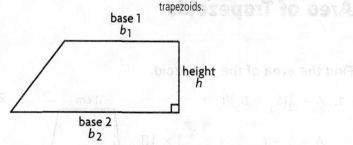

To find the area of a trapezoid, use the formula
Area $= \frac{1}{2} \times$ (base$_1$ + base$_2$) $\times$ height.

Find the area of the trapezoid.

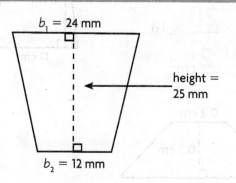

Step 1 Write the formula to find the area. $A = \frac{1}{2}(b_1 + b_2)h$

Step 2 Replace the variable b_1 with 24,
b_2 with 12, and h with 25. $A = \frac{1}{2} \times (24 + 12) \times 25$

Step 3 Use the order of operations to simplify. $A = \frac{1}{2} \times 36 \times 25$

$A = 18 \times 25$

$A = 450$

Step 4 Use the appropriate units. $A = 450$ mm^2

Find the area.

1.

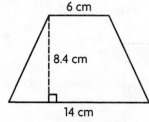

Write the formula. $A = $ _____

Replace the variables. $A = \frac{1}{2} \times ($ _____ + _____ $) \times$ _____

Simplify. $A = \frac{1}{2} \times$ _____ $\times$ _____

$A = $ _____

2.

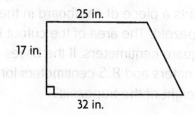

3.

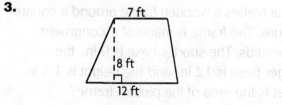

Area of Trapezoids

Find the area of the trapezoid.

1. $A = \frac{1}{2}(b_1 + b_2)h$

    $A = \frac{1}{2} + (\underline{\mathbf{11}} + \underline{\mathbf{17}}) \times 18$

    $A = \frac{1}{2} \times \underline{\mathbf{28}} \times 18$

    $A = \underline{\mathbf{252}}$ cm^2

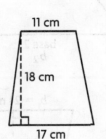

2.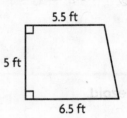

   $A =$ _____

3.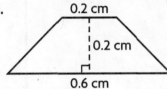

   $A =$ _____

4.

   $A =$ _____

Find the height of the trapezoid.

5.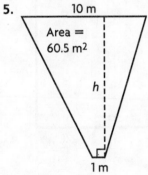

   $h =$ _____

6.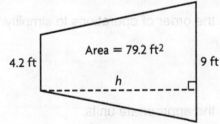

   $h =$ _____

Problem Solving REAL WORLD

7. Sonia makes a wooden frame around a square picture. The frame is made of 4 congruent trapezoids. The shorter base is 9 in., the longer base is 12 in., and the height is 1.5 in. What is the area of the picture frame?

    _____

8. Bryan cuts a piece of cardboard in the shape of a trapezoid. The area of the cutout is 43.5 square centimeters. If the bases are 6 centimeters and 8.5 centimeters long, what is the height of the trapezoid?

    _____

Name _____

Area of Regular Polygons

In a regular polygon, all sides have the same length and all angles have the same measure. To find the area of a regular polygon, divide it into triangles.

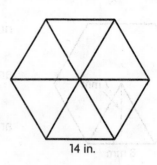

Step 1 Draw line segments from each vertex to the center of the regular polygon.

Step 2 Examine the figure.

The line segments divide the polygon into congruent triangles. This polygon is a hexagon. A hexagon has 6 sides, so there are 6 triangles.

Step 3 Find the area of one triangle. Use the formula $A = \frac{1}{2}bh$.

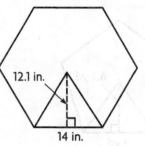

The base of the triangle (or one side of the hexagon) is 14 in. The height of the triangle is 12.1 in.

$A = \frac{1}{2} \times 14 \times 12.1 = \frac{1}{2} \times 169.4 = 84.7$ in.²

Step 4 Multiply by 6, because there are 6 triangles.

$84.7 \times 6 = 508.2$

So, the area of the regular hexagon is 508.2 square inches.

Find the area of the regular polygon.

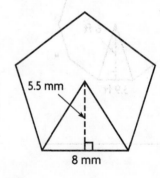

1. Number of congruent triangles inside the pentagon: _____

Area of each triangle:

$A = \frac{1}{2} \times$ _____ $\times 5.5 = \frac{1}{2} \times$ _____ $=$ _____ mm²

Area of the pentagon: _____ $\times$ _____ $=$ _____ mm²

2.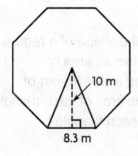

_____ m²

3.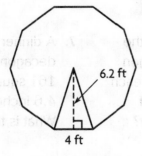

_____ ft²

4.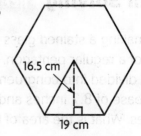

_____ cm²

Area of Regular Polygons

Find the area of the regular polygon.

1.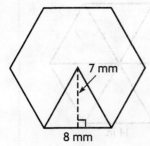

number of congruent triangles inside the figure: ____**6**____

area of each triangle: $\frac{1}{2} \times$ ____**8**____ $\times$ ____**7**____ $=$ ____**28**____ mm²

area of hexagon: ____**168 mm²**____

2.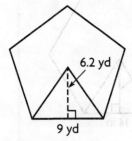

_____

3.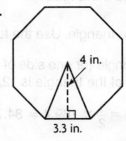

_____

4.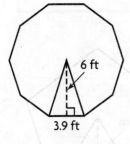

_____

5.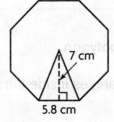

_____

Problem Solving

6. Stu is making a stained glass window in the shape of a regular pentagon. The pentagon can be divided into congruent triangles, each with a base of 8.7 inches and a height of 6 inches. What is the area of the window?

_____

7. A dinner platter is in the shape of a regular decagon. The platter has an area of 161 square inches and a side length of 4.6 inches. What is the area of each triangle? What is the height of each triangle?

_____

Composite Figures

A **composite figure** is made up of two or more simpler figures, such as triangles and quadrilaterals.

The composite figure shows the front view of a bird house. Complete Steps 1–4 to find the area of the shaded region.

Step 1 Find the area of the rectangle.

$A = lw = 16 \times$ _____ = _____ cm²

Step 2 Find the area of the triangle.

$A = \frac{1}{2}bh = \frac{1}{2} \times$ _____ $\times$ _____

$= \frac{1}{\underset{1}{\cancel{2}}} \times \frac{\overset{8}{\cancel{16}}}{1} \times$ _____ = _____ cm²

Step 3 Find the area of the square.

$A = s^2 = ($ _____ $)^2$

$=$ _____ cm²

Step 4 Add the areas of the rectangle and triangle. Then subtract the area of the square.

Shaded area = _____ + _____ − _____ = _____ cm²

So, the area of the shaded region is _____ cm².

(figure: bird house front view with labels 8 cm, 20 cm, 10 cm, 10 cm, 16 cm)

Find the area of the shaded region.

1.

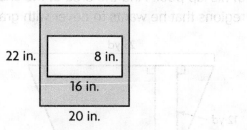

22 in.   8 in.
16 in.
20 in.

2.

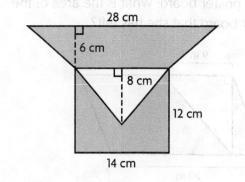

28 cm
6 cm
8 cm
12 cm
14 cm

Composite Figures

Find the area of the figure.

1.

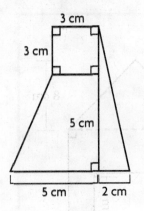

area of square $A = s \times s$

$= \underline{\ 3\ } \times \underline{\ 3\ } = \underline{\ 9\ } \ \text{cm}^2$

area of triangle $A = \frac{1}{2}bh$

$= \frac{1}{2} \times \underline{\ 2\ } \times \underline{\ 8\ } = \underline{\ 8\ } \ \text{cm}^2$

area of trapezoid $A = \frac{1}{2}(b_1 + b_2)h$

$= \frac{1}{2} \times (\underline{\ 5\ } + \underline{\ 3\ }) \times \underline{\ 5\ } = \underline{\ 20\ } \ \text{cm}^2$

area of composite figure

$A = \underline{\ 9\ } \ \text{cm}^2 + \underline{\ 8\ } \ \text{cm}^2 + \underline{\ 20\ } \ \text{cm}^2$

$= \underline{\ 37\ } \ \text{cm}^2$

2.

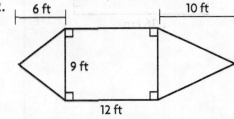

_____

3.

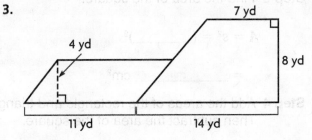

_____

Problem Solving

4. Janelle is making a poster. She cuts a triangle out of poster board. What is the area of the poster board that she has left?

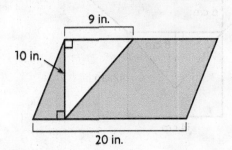

_____

5. Michael wants to place grass on the sides of his lap pool. Find the area of the shaded regions that he wants to cover with grass.

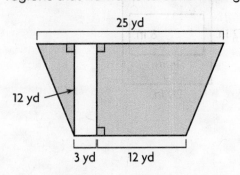

_____

Lesson 80

COMMON CORE STANDARD CC.6.G.1

Lesson Objective: Determine the effect of changing dimensions on the area of a polygon by using the strategy *find a pattern.*

Problem Solving • Changing Dimensions

Amy is sewing a quilt out of fabric pieces shaped like parallelograms. The smallest of the parallelograms is shown at the right. The dimensions of another parallelogram she is using can be found by multiplying the dimensions of the smallest parallelogram by 3. How do the areas of the parallelograms compare?

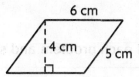

6 cm
4 cm
5 cm

Read the Problem		
What do I need to find? I need to find _____ _____ _____ _____ .	**What information do I need to use?** I need to use _____ _____ _____ _____ .	**How will I use the information?** I can draw a sketch of each _____ and calculate the _____ . Then I can _____ _____ .

Solve the Problem		
Sketch	**Multiplier**	**Area**
	none	$A = 6 \times$ ____ = ____ cm²
	3	$A =$ ____ $\times$ ____ = _____ cm²

When the dimensions are multiplied by 3, the area is multiplied by ____.

1. Sunni drew a parallelogram with area 20 in.². If she doubles the dimensions, what is the area of the new parallelogram?

_____

2. Abe drew a square with side length 20 mm. If he draws a new square with dimensions that are half that of the previous square, what is the area of the new square?

_____

Geometry

Problem Solving • Changing Dimensions

Read each problem and solve.

1. The dimensions of a 5-in. by 3-in. rectangle are multiplied by 6. How is the area affected?

   new dimensions: $l = 6 \times 5 = 30$ in.
   $w = 6 \times 3 = 18$ in.

   original area: $A = 5 \times 3 = 15$ in.^{2}

   new area: $A = 30 \times 18 = 540$ in.^{2}

   $\dfrac{\text{new area}}{\text{original area}} = \dfrac{540}{15} = 36$

   The area was multiplied by ___36___.

2. The dimensions of a 7-cm by 2-cm rectangle are multiplied by 3. How is the area affected?

   multiplied by _____

3. The dimensions of a 3-ft by 6-ft rectangle are multiplied by $\frac{1}{3}$. How is the area affected?

   multiplied by _____

4. The dimensions of a triangle with base 10 in. and height 4.8 in. are multiplied by 4. How is the area affected?

   multiplied by _____

5. The dimensions of a 1-yd by 9-yd rectangle are multiplied by 5. How is the area affected?

   multiplied by _____

6. The dimensions of a 4-in. square are multiplied by 3. How is the area affected?

   multiplied by _____

7. The dimensions of a triangle with base 1.5 m and height 6 m are multiplied by 2. How is the area affected?

   multiplied by _____

8. The dimensions of a triangle are multiplied by $\frac{1}{4}$. The area of the smaller triangle can be found by multiplying the area of the original triangle by what number?

   _____

Name _____

Lesson 81

COMMON CORE STANDARD CC.6.G.2
Lesson Objective: Investigate the volume
of rectangular prisms with fractional edge
lengths.

Fractions and Volume

Find the volume of a rectangular prism that is
$2\frac{1}{2}$ **units long, 2 units wide, and** $1\frac{1}{2}$ **units high.**

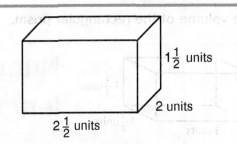

$1\frac{1}{2}$ units

2 units

$2\frac{1}{2}$ units

Step 1 Stack cubes with $\frac{1}{2}$-unit side length to form
a rectangular prism.

Length: 5 cubes = $\frac{1}{2} + \frac{1}{2} + \frac{1}{2} + \frac{1}{2} + \frac{1}{2} = 2\frac{1}{2}$ units

Width: 4 cubes = $\frac{1}{2} + \frac{1}{2} + \frac{1}{2} + \frac{1}{2} = 2$ units

Height: 3 cubes = $\frac{1}{2} + \frac{1}{2} + \frac{1}{2} = 1\frac{1}{2}$ units

Step 2 Count the total number of cubes.

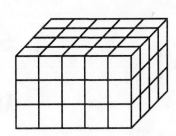

60 cubes

Step 3 It takes 8 cubes with $\frac{1}{2}$-unit side lengths to
make 1 unit cube. So, each smaller cube
has $\frac{1}{8}$ the volume of a unit cube.

Divide 60 by 8 to find how many unit cubes
it would take to form the prism. Write the
remainder as a fraction and simplify.

$60 \div 8 = 7\frac{4}{8}$ $7\frac{4}{8} = 7\frac{1}{2}$

So, the volume of the prism is $7\frac{1}{2}$ cubic units.

1. Find the volume of the rectangular prism.

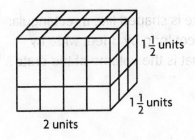

$1\frac{1}{2}$ units

$1\frac{1}{2}$ units

2 units

a. Stack cubes with $\frac{1}{2}$-unit side lengths to form the prism.

b. Count the cubes. _____

c. Divide by 8. _____ ÷ 8 = _____

d. The prism has a volume of _____ cubic units.

Name _____

Lesson 81

CC.6.G.2

Fractions and Volume

Find the volume of the rectangular prism.

1.

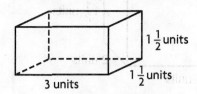

$1\frac{1}{2}$ units

$1\frac{1}{2}$ units

3 units

Number of cubes with side length $\frac{1}{2}$ unit: 54

$54 \div 8 = 6$ with a remainder of 6

$54 \div 8 = 6 + \frac{6}{8} = 6\frac{3}{4}$

Volume $= 6\frac{3}{4}$ cubic units

2.

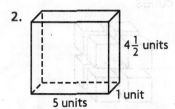

$4\frac{1}{2}$ units

1 unit

5 units

_____

3.

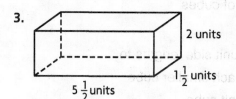

2 units

$1\frac{1}{2}$ units

$5\frac{1}{2}$ units

_____

4.

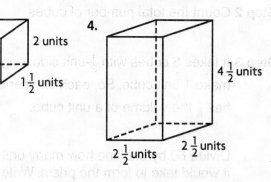

$4\frac{1}{2}$ units

$2\frac{1}{2}$ units

$2\frac{1}{2}$ units

_____

Problem Solving REAL WORLD

5. Miguel is pouring liquid into a container that is $4\frac{1}{2}$ inches long by $3\frac{1}{2}$ inches wide by 2 inches high. How many cubic inches of liquid will fit in the container?

6. A shipping crate is shaped like a rectangular prism. It is $5\frac{1}{2}$ feet long by 3 feet wide by 3 feet high. What is the volume of the crate?

_____

_____

162

© Houghton Mifflin Harcourt Publishing Company

Lesson 82

COMMON CORE STANDARD CC.6.G.2

Lesson Objective: Use formulas to find the volume of rectangular prisms with fractional edge lengths.

Algebra • Volume of Rectangular Prisms

You can find the volume of a prism by using the formula $V = Bh$. V stands for volume, B stands for the area of the base, and h stands for the height.

For a rectangular prism, any face can be the base, since all faces are rectangles.

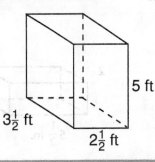

5 ft

$3\frac{1}{2}$ ft

$2\frac{1}{2}$ ft

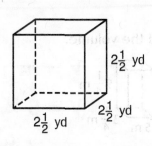

$2\frac{1}{2}$ yd

$2\frac{1}{2}$ yd

$2\frac{1}{2}$ yd

Find the volume of the rectangular prism.

Step 1 Find the area of the base.
The base is $2\frac{1}{2}$ ft by $3\frac{1}{2}$ ft.

$A = l \times w$

$A = 2\frac{1}{2}$ ft $\times 3\frac{1}{2}$ ft $= 8\frac{3}{4}$ ft²

So, the volume of the rectangular prism is $43\frac{3}{4}$ ft³.

Step 2 Multiply the area of the base by the height.

$V = Bh$

$V = 8\frac{3}{4}$ ft² $\times 5$ ft $= 43\frac{3}{4}$ ft³

Find the volume of the cube.

Step 1 Because the length, width, and height are all equal, you can use a special formula.

$V = Bh = l \times w \times h$

$V = s^3$

So, the volume of the cube is $15\frac{5}{8}$ yd³.

Step 2 Substitute $2\frac{1}{2}$ for s.

$V = s^3 = \left(2\frac{1}{2}\right)^3 = \left(\frac{5}{2}\right)^3$

$V = \frac{5}{2}$ yd $\times \frac{5}{2}$ yd $\times \frac{5}{2}$ yd $= \frac{125}{8}$ yd³

$= 15\frac{5}{8}$ yd³

Find the volume.

1.

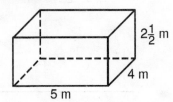

$2\frac{1}{2}$ m

4 m

5 m

2.

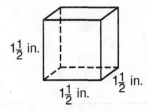

$1\frac{1}{2}$ in.

$1\frac{1}{2}$ in.

$1\frac{1}{2}$ in.

3.

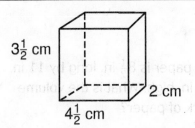

$3\frac{1}{2}$ cm

2 cm

$4\frac{1}{2}$ cm

4.

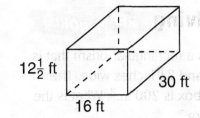

$12\frac{1}{2}$ ft

30 ft

16 ft

Volume of Rectangular Prisms

Find the volume.

1.

$V = lwh$

$V = 5 \times 3\frac{1}{4} \times 9\frac{1}{4}$

$V = 150\frac{5}{16}$ m³

$9\frac{1}{4}$ m
$3\frac{1}{4}$ m
5 m

2.

2 in.
$2\frac{1}{2}$ in.
$5\frac{1}{2}$ in.

3.

$4\frac{1}{2}$ mm
$4\frac{1}{2}$ mm
$4\frac{1}{2}$ mm

4.

6 ft
$2\frac{1}{2}$ ft
$7\frac{1}{2}$ ft

5.

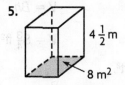

$4\frac{1}{2}$ m
8 m²

6.

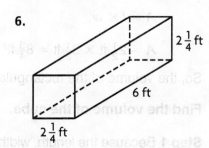

$2\frac{1}{4}$ ft
6 ft
$2\frac{1}{4}$ ft

7.

14 m
$7\frac{1}{4}$ m
$9\frac{1}{2}$ m

8.

$\frac{1}{3}$ in.
$\frac{1}{3}$ in.
$\frac{1}{3}$ in.

9.

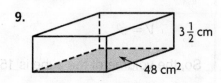

$3\frac{1}{2}$ cm
48 cm²

Problem Solving REAL WORLD

10. A cereal box is a rectangular prism that is 8 inches long and $2\frac{1}{2}$ inches wide. The volume of the box is 200 in.³. What is the height of the box?

11. A stack of paper is $8\frac{1}{2}$ in. long by 11 in. wide by 4 in. high. What is the volume of the stack of paper?

Lesson 83

COMMON CORE STANDARD CC.6.G.3

Lesson Objective: Plot polygons on a coordinate plane, and use coordinates to find side lengths.

Figures on the Coordinate Plane

The vertices of a parallelogram are $A(-2, 2)$, $B(-3, 5)$, $C(4, 5)$, and $D(5, 2)$.
Graph the parallelogram and find the length of side AD.

Step 1 Draw the parallelogram on the coordinate plane. Plot the points and then connect the points with straight lines.

Step 2 Find the length of side AD.

Horizontal distance of A from 0: $|-2| = 2$
Horizontal distance of D from 0: $|5| = 5$

Points A and D are in different quadrants, so add to find the distance from A to D.
$2 + 5 = 7$ units

So, the length of side AD is 7 units.

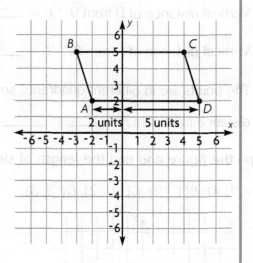

Graph the figure and find the length of the given side.

1. Triangle *JKL*
$J(-3, -3)$, $K(-3, 5)$, $L(5, 2)$

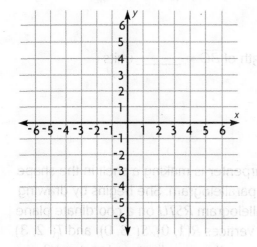

length of $\overline{JK}$ = _____

2. Trapezoid *WXYZ*
$W(-2, -3)$, $X(-2, 3)$, $Y(3, 5)$, $Z(3, -3)$

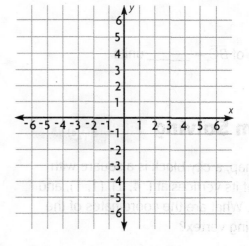

length of $\overline{WZ}$ = _____

Geometry

Figures on the Coordinate Plane

1. The vertices of triangle *DEF* are $D(^-2, 3)$, $E(3, ^-2)$, and $F(^-2, ^-2)$. Graph the triangle, and find the length of side $\overline{DF}$.

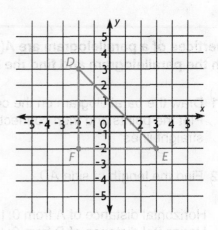

Vertical distance of *D* from 0: $|3| = $ __**3**__ units

Vertical distance of *F* from 0: $|^-2| = $ __**2**__ units

The points are in different quadrants, so add to find the

distance from *D* to *F*: __**3**__ + __**2**__ = __**5**__ units.

Graph the figure and find the length of side $\overline{BC}$.

2. $A(1, 4)$, $B(1, ^-2)$, $C(^-3, ^-2)$, $D(^-3, 3)$

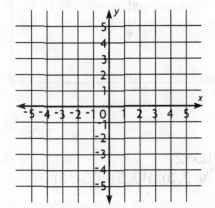

Length of $\overline{BC} = $ _____ units

3. $A(^-1, 4)$, $B(5, 4)$, $C(5, 1)$, $D(^-1, 1)$

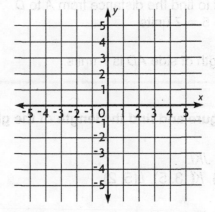

Length of $\overline{BC} = $ _____ units

Problem Solving REAL WORLD

4. On a map, a city block is a square with three of its vertices at $(^-4, 1)$, $(1, 1)$, and $(1, ^-4)$. What are the coordinates of the remaining vertex?

5. A carpenter is making a shelf in the shape of a parallelogram. She begins by drawing parallelogram *RSTU* on a coordinate plane with vertices $R(1, 0)$, $S(^-3, 0)$, and $T(^-2, 3)$. What are the coordinates of vertex *U*?

Three-Dimensional Figures and Nets

Solid figures have three dimensions—length, width, and height. They can be named by the shapes of their bases, the number of bases, and the shapes of their lateral faces.

Identify and draw a net for the solid figure.

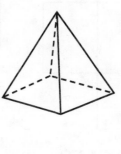 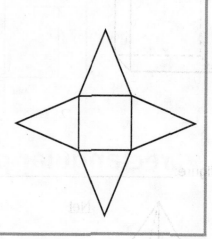

Step 1 Describe the base of the figure.
The base is a square.

Step 2 Describe the lateral surfaces.
The lateral surfaces are triangles.

So, the figure is a square pyramid.

Step 3 Name the shapes to be used in the net. Then make a sketch. Draw a square for the base, and four triangles for the lateral faces.

Identify and draw a net for the solid figure.

1.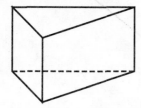

2.

figure: _____

figure: _____

Name _____

Three-Dimensional Figures and Nets

Identify and draw a net for the solid figure.

1. 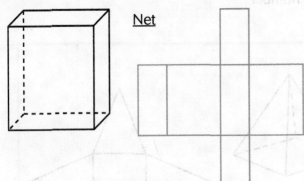   Net

figure: **rectangular prism** _____

2. 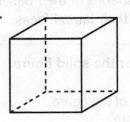   Net

figure: _____

3. 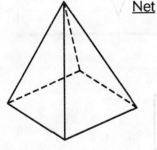   Net

figure: _____

4. 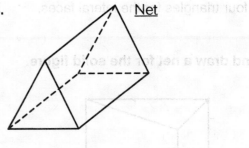   Net

figure: _____

Problem Solving REAL WORLD

5. Hobie's Candies are sold in triangular-pyramid-shaped boxes. How many triangles are needed to make one box?

6. Nina used plastic rectangles to make 6 rectangular prisms. How many rectangles did she use?

_____

_____

Lesson 85

COMMON CORE STANDARD CC.6.G.4

Lesson Objective: Use nets to recognize that the surface area of a prism is equal to the sum of the areas of its faces.

Explore Surface Area Using Nets

The net of a solid figure shows you all of the faces or surfaces of the figure. A net can help you find the **surface area** of a figure.

Find the surface area of the rectangular prism.

1 in.
2 in.
4 in.

E
A C B D
F

Step 1 Make a net of the rectangular prism. The prism has 6 rectangular faces, so the net has 6 rectangles.

Step 2 Find the area of each face of the prism.

First Way: Count the grid squares on each rectangle to find its area.

Second Way: Calculate the area of each rectangle by multiplying *length* × *width*.

A: 8 squares	$4 \times 2 = 8$
B: 8 squares	$4 \times 2 = 8$
C: 4 squares	$4 \times 1 = 4$
D: 4 squares	$4 \times 1 = 4$
E: 2 squares	$2 \times 1 = 2$
F: 2 squares	$2 \times 1 = 2$

Step 3 Add the areas of all the rectangular faces.

28 squares   28 square inches

So, the surface area of the rectangular prism is 28 square inches (in.²).

Use the net to find the surface area of the prism.

1.

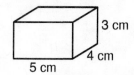

3 cm
4 cm
5 cm

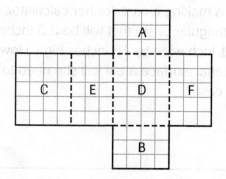

A
C E D F
B

a. Find the area of each face.

A: _____   B: _____

C: _____   D: _____

E: _____   F: _____

b. Add: A + B + C + D + E + F = _____

c. The surface area is _____ cm².

Geometry

Explore Surface Area Using Nets

Use the net to find the surface area of the
rectangular prism.

1.
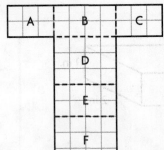

A: 6 squares

B: 8 squares

C: 6 squares

D: 12 squares

E: 8 squares

F: 12 squares

2.
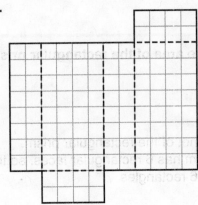

52 square units

Find the surface area of the rectangular prism.

3.
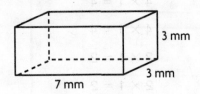

4.
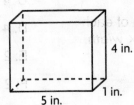

5.
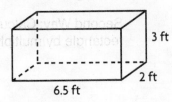

_____

_____

_____

Problem Solving REAL WORLD

6. Jeremiah is covering a cereal box with fabric
for a school project. If the box is 6 inches long
by 2 inches wide by 14 inches high, how much
surface area does Jeremiah have to cover?

_____

7. Tia is making a case for her calculator. It is a
rectangular prism that will be 3.5 inches long
by 1 inch wide by 10 inches high. How much
material (surface area) will she need to make
the case?

_____

Lesson 86

COMMON CORE STANDARD CC.6.G.4
Lesson Objective: Find the surface area of prisms.

Algebra • Surface Area of Prisms

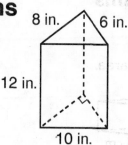

You can find the surface area of a figure by adding the lateral surface area to the sum of the areas of the bases.

Use a net to find the surface area.

Step 1 Draw a net.

Note any faces that have equal areas.

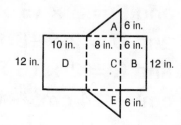

Step 2 Both triangular bases have the same area.

Base A: $A = \frac{1}{2} bh = \frac{1}{2} \times 6 \times 8 = 24$ in.^{2}

Base E: $A = 24$ in.^{2}

Step 3 Find the areas of the rectangular faces.

Face B: $A = lw = 6 \times 12 = 72$ in.^{2}

Face C: $A = lw = 8 \times 12 = 96$ in.^{2}

Face D: $A = lw = 10 \times 12 = 120$ in.^{2}

Step 4 Add the areas: A + B + C + D + E

$24 + 72 + 96 + 120 + 24 = 336$ in.^{2}

So, the surface area of the triangular prism is 336 square inches (in.^{2}).

Use a net to find the surface area.

1.

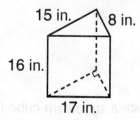

2.

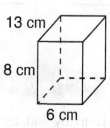

_____   _____

3.

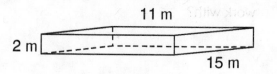

4.

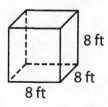

_____   _____

Name _____

Name _____

Lesson 86

CC.6.G.4

Surface Area of Prisms

Use a net to find the surface area.

1.

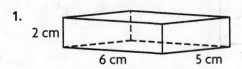

Area of A and F = $2 \times (5 \times 2) = 20$ cm^2
Area of B and D = $2 \times (6 \times 2) = 24$ cm^2
Area of C and E = $2 \times (6 \times 5) = 60$ cm^2
S.A. = 20 cm^2 + 24 cm^2 + 60 cm^2 = 104 cm^2

2.

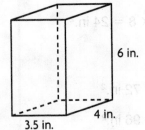

3.

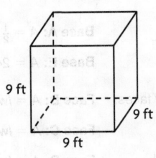

4.

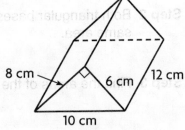

_____ _____ _____

Problem Solving REAL WORLD

5. A shoe box measures 15 in. by 7 in. by $4\frac{1}{2}$ in. What is the surface area of the box?

6. Vivian is working with a styrofoam cube for art class. The length of one side is 5 inches. How much surface area does Vivian have to work with?

_____ _____

172

© Houghton Mifflin Harcourt Publishing Company

Algebra • Surface Area of Pyramids

To find the surface area of a pyramid, add the area of the base to the **lateral area**. The lateral area is the combined area of the triangular faces.

Find the surface area of the square pyramid.

Step 1 The base is a square with side length of 6 in. Use the formula $A = s^2$ to find the area. Substitute 6 for the variable s.

$A = 6^2 = 36$ in.^{2}

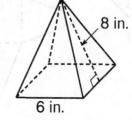

8 in.

6 in.

Step 2 The lateral faces are four triangles with base of 6 in. and height of 8 in. Find the area of one triangular lateral face using the formula $A = \frac{1}{2}bh$. Substitute 6 for b and 8 for h.

$A = \frac{1}{2}(6)(8) = 24$ in.^{2}

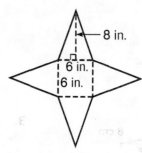

8 in.

6 in.
6 in.

Step 3 Multiply by 4 to find the total lateral area. $L = 24 \times 4 = 96$ in.^{2}

Step 4 Add the area of the base and the lateral area. $S = 36$ in.$^2 + 96$ in.$^2 = 132$ in.^{2}

So, the surface area of the square pyramid is 132 square inches (in.^{2}).

Use a net to find the surface area of the square pyramid.

1.

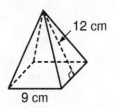

12 cm

9 cm

a. Area of the base: _____

b. Area of one triangular lateral face:

_____

c. Total lateral area: _____

d. Total surface area: _____

2.

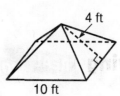

4 ft

10 ft

a. Area of the base: _____

b. Area of one triangular lateral face:

_____

c. Total lateral area: _____

d. Total surface area: _____

Geometry

Surface Area of Pyramids

Use a net to find the surface area of the square pyramid.

1.

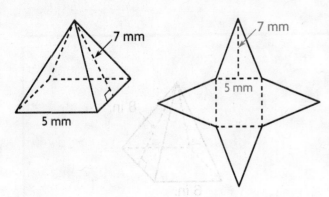

Base: $A = 5^2 = 25$ mm^2

Face: $A = \frac{1}{2}(5)(7)$

$\quad\quad = 17.5$ mm^2

S.A. $= 25 + 4 \times 17.5$

$\quad\quad = 25 + 70$

$\quad\quad = 95$ mm^2

2.

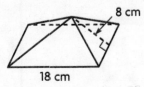

_____

3.

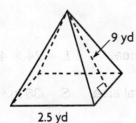

_____

4.

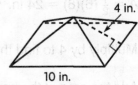

_____

Problem Solving

5. Cho is building a sandcastle in the shape of a triangular pyramid. The area of the base is 7 square feet. Each side of the base has a length of 4 feet and the height of each face is 2 feet. What is the surface area of the pyramid?

_____

6. The top of a skyscraper is shaped like a square pyramid. Each side of the base has a length of 60 meters and the height of each triangle is 20 meters. What is the lateral area of the pyramid?

_____

Lesson 88
COMMON CORE STANDARD CC.6.G.4

Lesson Objective: Solve problems involving area, surface area, and volume by applying the strategy *use a formula*.

Problem Solving • Geometric Measurements

Leslie stores gardening supplies in this shed shaped like a rectangular prism. What is the area of the ground covered by the shed?

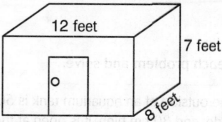

12 feet

7 feet

8 feet

Read the Problem	Solve the Problem
What do I need to find? I need to find _____ _____ _____.	Choose the measure—area, surface area, or volume—that gives the area of the ground covered by the barrel. Explain. _____ _____ _____ _____
What information do I need to use? I need to use _____ _____.	Choose an appropriate formula.
How will I use the information? First, I will decide _____ _____. Then I will choose a _____ I can use to calculate this measure. Finally, I will _____ _____ _____	Replace the variables *l* and *w* in the area formula with their values in the dimensions of the shed. $l =$ _____ ft $w =$ _____ ft Evaluate the formula. $A =$ _____ $\times$ _____ $=$ _____ ft²

Solve.

1. Leslie is covering bricks with paint. Each brick is 8 in. long, 4 in. wide, and 2 in. high. How many square inches will Leslie paint on each brick?

_____

2. Leslie's planting box is shaped like a rectangular prism. It is 60 cm long, 35 cm wide, and 40 cm high. How many cubic cm of soil will Leslie need to fill the box?

_____

Problem Solving • Geometric Measurements

Read each problem and solve.

1. The outside of an aquarium tank is 50 cm long, 50 cm wide, and 30 cm high. It is open at the top. The glass used to make the tank is 1 cm thick. How much water can the tank hold?

   $l = 50 - 2 = 48, w = 50 - 2 = 48,$
   $h = 30 - 1 = 29$
   $V = l \times w \times h$
   $\quad = 48 \times 48 \times 29$
   $\quad = 66,816$

   _____ $66,816 \text{ cm}^3$

2. Arnie keeps his pet snake in an open-topped glass cage. The outside of the cage is 73 cm long, 60 cm wide, and 38 cm high. The glass used to make the cage is 0.5 cm thick. What is the inside volume of the cage?

   _____

3. A gift box measures 14 in. by 12 in. by 6 in. How much wrapping paper is needed to exactly cover the box?

   _____

4. A display number cube measures 20 in. on a side. The sides are numbered 1–6. The odd-numbered sides are covered in blue fabric and the even-numbered sides are covered in red fabric. How much red fabric was used?

   _____

5. The caps on the tops of staircase posts are shaped like square pyramids. The side length of the base of each cap is 4 inches. The height of the face of each cap is 5 inches. What is the surface area of the caps for two posts?

   _____

6. A water irrigation tank is shaped like a cube and has a side length of $2\frac{1}{2}$ feet. How many cubic feet of water are needed to completely fill the tank?

   _____

Recognize Statistical Questions

A **statistical question** is a question about a set of **data** that can vary. To answer a statistical question, you need to collect or look at a set of data.

Identify the statistical questions about Jack's homework time.

A. How many times did Jack spend longer than an hour on homework this week?
Statistical question. Jack is unlikely to do homework for the same amount of time each day, so the question asks about a set of data that can vary. You could answer it with data about Jack's homework time for a week.

B. How long did Jack do homework today?
Not a statistical question. It asks about Jack's homework time on one day. It does not refer to a set of data that varies.

Write a statistical question about your school's cafeteria.

Think of what kind of data could vary in the situation. In this situation, it might be menu items, students, or activities.

These are both statistical questions:

A. How many students were in the cafeteria during fourth period each day for the past two weeks?

B. What was the greatest number of entrees served in one day in the cafeteria last month?

Identify the statistical question. Circle the letter of the question.

1. **A.** How many people flew from New York to San Francisco yesterday?
   B. How many people flew from New York to San Francisco each day this month?

2. **A.** How many siblings does each of your classmates have?
   B. How many siblings does your best friend have?

Write a statistical question you could ask in the situation.

3. Hannah recorded the temperature in her yard every day for a week.

   _____

4. Ian knows his scores for each time he has bowled this year.

   _____

Statistics and Probability

Recognize Statistical Questions

Identify the statistical question. Explain your reasoning.

1. **A.** How many touchdowns did the quarterback throw during the last game of the season?

   B. How many touchdowns did the quarterback throw each game of the season?

   B; the number of touchdowns in each game can vary.

2. **A.** What was the score in the first frame of a bowling game?

   B. What are the scores in 10 frames of a bowling game?

   _____
   _____
   _____

3. **A.** How many hours of television did you watch each day this week?

   B. How many hours of television did you watch on Saturday?

   _____
   _____
   _____

Write a statistical question you could ask in the situation.

4. A teacher recorded the test scores of her students.

   _____
   _____

5. A car salesman knows how many of each model of a car was sold in a month.

   _____
   _____

Problem Solving  REAL WORLD

6. The city tracked the amount of waste that was recycled from 2000 to 2007. Write a statistical question about the situation.

   _____
   _____
   _____

7. The daily low temperature is recorded for a week. Write a statistical question about the situation.

   _____
   _____
   _____

Lesson 90

COMMON CORE STANDARD CC.6.SP.2
Lesson Objective: Describe the distribution of a data set collected to answer a statistical question.

Describe Distributions

When interpreting data, it helps to make a graph and then analyze the distribution of data.

Mr. Chen asked all of his students how long it takes them to clean their rooms. He displayed the information in a histogram. Describe the data distribution.

Minutes Spent Cleaning Rooms

Step 1 Look for clusters.	There are no groups of data that are separated from the rest, so there are no clusters of data.
Step 2 Look for gaps.	There are no intervals that contain no data, so there are no gaps in the data.
Step 3 Look for peaks.	There is one peak, at the interval 41–60.
Step 4 Look for symmetry.	Imagine folding the graph in half vertically, along the interval 41–60. The halves are not identical, but they are close. The graph has symmetry.

1. Sally has a restaurant. She recorded the cost of each person's dinner on Friday. Describe the distribution.

   _____

   _____

   _____

   _____

   _____

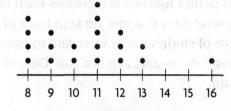

Cost (in dollars) of Dinners Ordered Friday

© Houghton Mifflin Harcourt Publishing Company

Describe Distributions

Chase asked people how many songs they have
bought online in the past month. Use the histogram of
the data he collected for 1–6.

1. What statistical question could Chase ask
   about the data?
   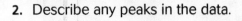
   Possible answer: What is the median
   number of songs purchased?

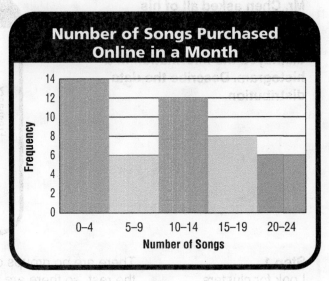

2. Describe any peaks in the data.

   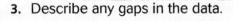

   _____

3. Describe any gaps in the data.

   _____

   _____

4. Does the graph have symmetry? Explain your reasoning.

   _____

   _____

Problem Solving REAL WORLD

5. Mr. Carpenter teaches five classes each day.
   For several days in a row, he kept track of the
   number of students who were late to class and
   displayed the results in a dot plot. Describe
   the data.

   _____

   _____

   _____

   _____

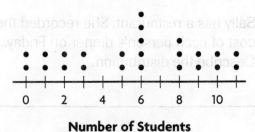

**Number of Students
Late to Class Each Day**

Problem Solving • Misleading Statistics

Zaire wants to move to a town where the annual snowfall is no more than 5 inches. A real estate agent tells her that the mean annual snowfall in a certain town is 4.5 inches. Other statistics about the town are given in the table. Does this location match what Zaire wants? Why or why not?

Town Statistics for Annual Snowfall (in.)	
Minimum	0.5
Maximum	12
Median	8
Mean	4.5

Read the Problem

What do I need to find?	**What information do I need to use?**	**How will I use the information?**
I need to decide if the annual snowfall in the town is _____ _____ .	I need the _____ in the table.	I will work backward from the statistics to draw conclusions about the _____ .

Solve the Problem

The minimum annual snowfall is _____

The maximum annual snowfall is _____

The median annual snowfall is _____

The mean annual snowfall is _____

Think: The median is _____, which means that half of the data is equal to or greater than _____ .

So, the annual snowfall is usually _____ than 5 inches because

at least half of the annual snowfall values are _____ than 5 inches. This location does not match what Zaire wants.

---

1. Mack says he typically spends 4 hours per week practicing his piano. For the past 6 weeks, he has practiced for 1, 1, 1, 2, 10, and 9 hours. Do you agree with Mack? Explain.

_____

_____

_____

Name _____

Problem Solving • Misleading Statistics

Mr. Jackson wants to make dinner reservations at a restaurant that has most meals costing less than $16. The Waterside Inn advertises that they have meals that average $15. The table shows the menu items.

Menu Items	
Meal	**Price**
Potato Soup	$6
Chicken	$16
Steak	$18
Pasta	$16
Shrimp	$18
Crab Cake	$19

1. What is the minimum price and maximum price?

   min = _____ $6

   max = _____ $19

2. What is the mean of the prices? _____

3. Construct a box plot for the data.

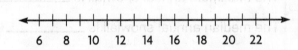

4. What is the range of the prices? _____

5. What is the interquartile range of the prices? _____

6. What is the median of the prices? _____

7. Does the menu match Mr. Jackson's requirements? Explain your reasoning.

   _____

   _____

   _____

Apply Measures of Center and Variability

You can use measures of center and variability to compare sets of data.

Two math groups were given the same test.

Test Scores		
	Mean	Interquartile range
Group A	76.9	30
Group B	81.1	8

Compare the data.

Step 1 Compare the means.

Group B's scores are higher on average than Group A's scores because it has a greater mean.

Step 2 Compare the interquartile ranges.

Group B has a smaller interquartile range, which means their scores do not vary as much as Group A's scores.

Compare the data.

1.

Bowling Scores		
	Median	Range
Team X	66	11
Team Y	70	19

2.

Cantaloupes Weights in Pounds		
	Mean	Range
Farm 1	4	1.5
Farm 2	7	3

_____

_____

_____

_____

_____

_____

Name _____

Apply Measures of Center and Variability

Solve.

1. The table shows temperature data for two cities. Use the information in the table to compare the data.

Daily High Temperatures (°F)		
	Mean	Interquartile Range
City 1	60	7
City 2	70	15

The mean of City 1's temperatures is _**less than**_ the mean of City 2's temperatures.

The _**interquartile range**_ of City 1's temperatures is _**less than**_ the _**interquartile range**_ of City 2's temperatures.

So, City 2 is typically _**warmer than**_ City 1, but City 2's temperatures vary _**more than**_ City 1's temperatures.

2. The table shows weights of fish that were caught in two different lakes. Find the median and range of each data set, and use these measures to compare the data.

Fish Weight (pounds)
Lake A: 7, 9, 10, 4, 6, 12
Lake B: 6, 7, 4, 5, 6, 4

_____

_____

_____

_____

Problem Solving REAL WORLD

3. Mrs. Mack measured the heights of her students in two classes. Class 1 has a median height of 130 cm and an interquartile range of 5 cm. Class 2 has a median height of 134 cm and an interquartile range of 8 cm. Write a statement that compares the data.

_____

_____

_____

_____

4. Richard's science test scores are 76, 80, 78, 84, and 80. His math test scores are 100, 80, 73, 94, and 71. Compare the medians and interquartile ranges.

_____

_____

_____

_____

Lesson 93

COMMON CORE STANDARD CC.6.SP.4

Lesson Objective: Display data in dot plots and frequency tables.

Dot Plots and Frequency Tables

A **dot plot** displays data by placing dots above a number line.
Each dot represents one data value.

Paloma sells produce at the farmers' market. The chart shows the number of pounds she sells each day. What was the most common number of pounds that Paloma sold?

Produce Sold (pounds)			
15	19	15	16
20	16	17	20
11	12	15	20
15	13	11	15

Step 1 Draw a number line with an appropriate scale. The chart contains numbers from 11 to 20, so use a scale from 10 to 20.

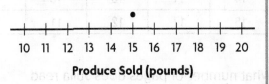

Step 2 For each data value in the chart, plot a dot above the number on the number line. The first data value in the chart is 15, so the dot is placed above 15 on the number line.

Complete the dot plot for the other values in the table. Since there are 16 data values, there should be 16 dots in all.

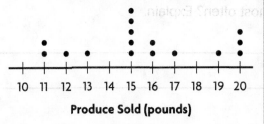

Step 3 The number of pounds Paloma sells most often is the value with the most dots. The stack with the most dots is at 15 pounds.

So, Paloma most often sells 15 pounds of produce.

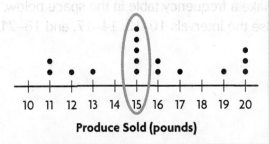

Use the data in the chart at right.

1. Complete the dot plot.

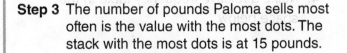

Number of Cars Sold per Month

Number of Cars Sold per Month					
26	32	35	29	30	26
25	29	28	31	29	26
35	26	26	28	26	30

2. What is the most common number of cars sold per month?

_____

Dot Plots and Frequency Tables

For 1–4, use the chart.

1. The chart shows the number of pages of a novel that Julia reads each day. Complete the dot plot using the data in the table.

Pages Read				
12	14	12	18	20
15	15	19	12	15
14	11	13	18	15
15	17	12	11	15

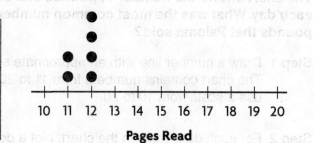

Pages Read

2. What number of pages does Julia read most often? Explain.

_____

_____

3. Make a frequency table in the space below. Use the intervals 10–13, 14–17, and 18–21.

4. Make a relative frequency table in the space below.

Problem Solving REAL WORLD

5. The frequency table shows the ages of the actors in a youth theater group. What percent of the actors are 10 to 12 years old?

_____

Actors in a Youth Theater Group	
Age	Frequency
7–9	8
10–12	22
13–15	10

Lesson 94

COMMON CORE STANDARD CC.6.SP.4
Lesson Objective: Display data in histograms.

Histograms

A **histogram** looks like a bar graph without spaces between bars. When you have data to organize, it is helpful to group the data into intervals and let each bar show the frequency, or number of data, in that interval.

Complete the frequency table below, using the data to the right. Then make a histogram.

Number of Hours of TV Watching per Week				
4	14	24	17	10
21	21	15	20	23
5	22	19	18	8
24	19	20	22	24

Step 1 Sort the data into each interval.
Only the 4 (1 item) is in the interval 1–4.
8 and 5 (2 items) are in 5–9.
10 and 14 (2 items) are in 10–14.
17, 15, 19, 18, 19 (5 items) are in 15–19.
24, 21, 21, 20, 23, 22, 24, 20, 22, 24 (10 items) are in 20–24.

Hours of TV/week	1–4	5–9	10–14	15–19	20–24
Frequency	1	2	2	5	10

Step 2 Check that all 20 items in the table are in the frequency table by adding.
$1 + 2 + 2 + 5 + 10 = 20$

Step 3 Make the histogram of the data.
Use a vertical scale from 0 to 12.
Title and label the histogram.
Draw a bar for each interval.
Draw bars the same width.
Draw the bar as high as the frequency.

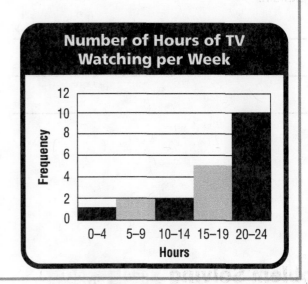

For 1–2, use the table shown.

Minutes on Treadmill Each Day				
28	28	24	52	35
43	29	34	55	21
38	60	71	59	62
19	64	39	70	55

1. Complete the frequency table of the data.

Number of Minutes	0–19	20–39	40–59	60–79
Frequency				

2. Make a histogram of the data.

Statistics and Probability

Histograms

For 1–4 use the data at right.

1. Complete the histogram for the data.

2. What do the numbers on the *y*-axis represent?

   _____

3. How many students scored from 60 to 69?

4. Use your histogram to find the number of students who got a score of 80 or greater. Explain.

   _____

   _____

   _____

Scores on a Math Test									
85	87	69	90	82	75	74	76	84	87
99	65	75	76	83	87	91	83	92	69

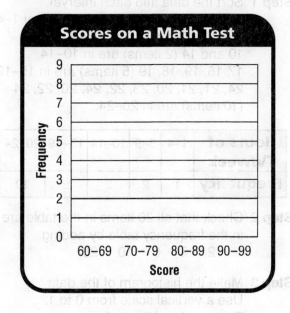

Scores on a Math Test

Problem Solving REAL WORLD

For 5–6, use the histogram.

5. For which two age groups are there the same number of customers?

   _____

6. How many customers are in the restaurant? How do you know?

   _____

   _____

   _____

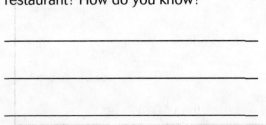

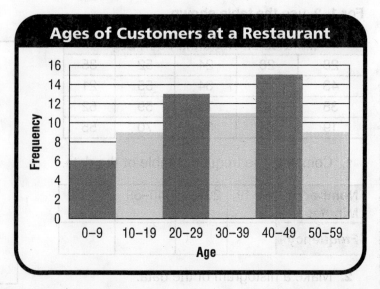

Ages of Customers at a Restaurant

Lesson Objective: Solve problems involving data by using the strategy *draw a diagram*.

Problem Solving •
Data Displays

The table shows the highest state populations in 2007, rounded to the nearest million. What percent of the states had at least 15 million residents?

2007 State Populations (in millions)					
18	10	6	9	6	9
6	37	13	12	6	11
24	8	6	6	19	6
10	6				

Read the Problem

What do I need to find?	What information do I need to use?	How will I use the information?
I need to find the _____ that had at least _____ million people.	I will use the _____ _____.	I will pick _____ for the data, find the _____ for each interval and use the frequencies to make a _____. I will use the information from the histogram to find a _____.

Solve the Problem

Make a frequency table.

Millions	5–9	10–14	15–19	20–24	25–29	30–34	35–40
Frequency			2			0	

Use the frequency table to make a _____.

States with at least 15 million: 2 + ___ + ___ = ___

Total states: 20

Percent with at least 15 million: $\dfrac{\square}{20}$ = ___ = ___%

So, ___ of the states have populations over 15 million.

2007 Population of States

Histogram with y-axis "Frequency" (0, 2, 4, 6, 8, 10, 12) and x-axis "Population (in millions)" (5–9, 10–14, 15–19, 20–24, 25–29, 30–34, 35–40)

Use the data in the histogram above.

1. What percent of the states had between 5 million and 14 million residents?

States with 5–14 million: _____

Percent with 5–14 million: _____ %

2. What percent of the states had less than 10 million residents?

States with less than 10 million: _____

Percent with less than 10 million: _____ %

Problem Solving • Data Displays

Read each problem and solve.

1. Josie collected data on the number of siblings her classmates have. Make a data display and determine the percent of Josie's classmates that have more than 2 siblings.

   5, 1, 2, 1, 2, 4, 3, 2, 2, 6

   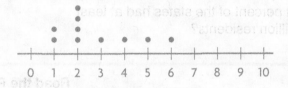

   40%

2. The following data show the number of field goals a kicker attempted each game. Make a data display and tell which number of field goals is the mode.

   4, 6, 2, 1, 3, 1, 2, 1, 5, 2, 2, 3

3. The math exam scores for a class are shown below. Make a data display. What percent of the scores are 90 and greater?

   91, 68, 83, 75, 81, 99, 97, 80, 85, 70, 89, 92, 77, 95, 100, 64, 88, 96, 76, 88

4. The heights of students in a class are shown below in inches. Make a data display. What percent of the students are taller than 62 inches?

   63, 57, 60, 64, 59, 62, 65, 58, 63, 65, 58, 61, 63, 64

5. The ages of employees are shown below. Which age is the mode?

   21, 18, 17, 19, 18, 23, 18, 16, 22, 18, 21, 18

Box Plots

The weights in ounces of 12 kittens are 20, 18, 22, 15, 17, 25, 25, 23, 13, 18, 16, and 22.

A **box plot** for the data would show how the values are spread out.

Make a box plot for the data.

Step 1 Write the numbers in order from least to greatest. Find the median and the least and greatest values.

13 15 16 17 18 (18 20) 22 22 23 25 25

Since there is an even number of values, the median is the mean of the two middle values. The median is 19. The least value is 13, and the greatest value is 25.

Step 2 Find the lower and upper quartiles.

The **lower quartile** is the median of the lower half of the data.

The **upper quartile** is the median of the upper half of the data.

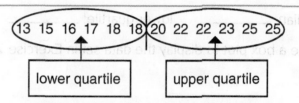

Draw a line where the median should be. Now the data set has been split into halves. (If there were an odd number of values in the data set, the median would be one of the data values, but you would not include it in the upper or lower half.) The lower quartile is 16.5, and the upper quartile is 22.5.

Step 3 Plot the five points on a number line, and construct the box and whiskers. Use an appropriate scale.

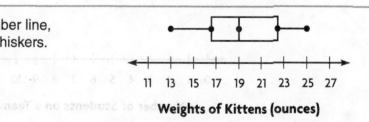

Weights of Kittens (ounces)

The numbers of laps completed on a track are 4, 5, 2, 7, 6, 8, 9, 8, and 6.
Use the data for 1–4.

1. What is the median? _____

2. What is the lower quartile? _____

3. What is the upper quartile? _____

4. Make a box plot for the data.

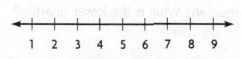

Number of Laps Completed

Statistics and Probability

Box Plots

Find the median, lower quartile, and upper quartile of the data.

1. the amounts of juice in 12 glasses, in fluid ounces:

    11, 8, 4, 9, 12, 14, 9, 16, 15, 11, 10, 7

    Order the data from least to greatest: **4, 7, 8, 9, 9, 10, 11, 11, 12, 14, 15, 16**

    median: **10.5**   lower quartile: **8.5**   upper quartile: **13**

2. the lengths of 10 pencils, in centimeters:

    18, 15, 4, 9, 14, 17, 16, 6, 8, 10

    median: _____   lower quartile: _____   upper quartile: _____

3. Make a box plot to display the data set in Exercise 2.

Lengths of Pencils (centimeters)

4. The numbers of students on several teams are 9, 4, 5, 10, 11, 9, 8, and 6. Make a box plot for the data.

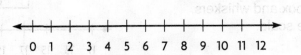

Number of Students on a Team

Problem Solving REAL WORLD

5. The amounts spent at a gift shop today are $19, $30, $28, $22, $20, $26, and $26. What is the median? What is the lower quartile?

6. The weights of six puppies in ounces are 8, 5, 7, 5, 6, and 9. What is the upper quartile of the data?

_____   _____

Lesson **97**

COMMON CORE STANDARDS CC.6.SP.5a, CC.6.SP.5b

Lesson Objective: Describe a data set by stating what quantity was measured and how it was measured.

Describe Data Collection

To describe a set of data, describe these features:

Attribute: the characteristic being recorded or measured
Unit: the unit of measurement, such as inches or grams
Means: the tool used for the observations or measurements
Observations: the number of observations or measurements

Describe the data set shown in the chart.

Step 1 What attribute is measured?
The attribute is *length of time* spent walking a dog.

Step 2 What unit of measurement is used?
The time is shown in *minutes.*

Step 3 What means was likely used to obtain the measurements?
To measure time, you use a *clock, timer,* or *stopwatch.*

Step 4 How many observations were made?
Count the number or observations: 8

Daily Dog Walks

Day	Time (min)	Day	Time (min)
1	35	5	60
2	40	6	25
3	25	7	90
4	55	8	20

Describe the data set by listing the attribute measured, the unit of measure, the likely means of measurement, and the number of observations.

1. Attribute: _____

Unit of measurement: _____

Means: _____

Number of observations: _____

Pet Weights (lb)

5.2	8	9.5	48.4	0.9
4.7	10.5	32	18	12

2. Attribute: _____

Unit of measurement: _____

Means: _____

Number of observations: _____

Serving Volume (cups)

Lettuce	2	Soup	1.5
Cheese	0.25	Ice Cream	0.75
Sauce	0.5		

Describe Data Collection

Describe the data set by listing the attribute measured, the unit of measure, the likely means of measurement, and the number of observations.

1. Daily temperature

Daily High Temperature (°F)				
78	83	72	65	70
76	75	71	80	75
73	74	81	79	69
81	78	76	80	82
70	77	74	71	73

Attribute: daily temperature;

unit of measure: degrees

Fahrenheit; means of

measurement: thermometer;

number of observations: 25

2. Plant heights

Height of Plants (inches)				
10.3	9.7	6.4	8.1	11.2
5.7	11.7	7.5	9.6	6.9

_____

_____

_____

_____

3. Cereal in boxes

Amount of Cereal in Boxes (cups)							
8	7	8.5	5	5	5	6.5	6
8	8.5	7	7	9	8	8	9

_____

_____

4. Dog weights

Weight of Dogs (pounds)							
22	17	34	23	19	18	20	20

_____

_____

_____

_____

Problem Solving REAL WORLD

5. The table below gives the amount of time Preston spends on homework. Name the likely means of measurement.

Amount of Time Spent on Homework (hours)							
5	3	1	2	4	1	3	2

_____

6. The table below shows the speed of cars on a highway. Name the unit of measure.

Speeds of Cars (miles per hour)							
71	55	53	65	68	61	59	62
70	69	57	50	56	66	67	63

_____

Mean as Fair Share and Balance Point

Five students brought 3, 4, 5, 3, and 5 cups of flour to the cooking club.
They divided it evenly so that each student got the same amount for cooking.
Use counters to show how many cups each student got.

Step 1 Make 5 stacks of counters: one stack for each student.

Use one counter for each cup of flour.

Step 2 Take counters from taller stacks and put them on shorter stacks. Move counters until all the stacks are the same height.

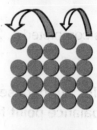

Step 3 Count the counters in each stack. There are **4** counters in each stack.

So, 4 is the mean of the data. When you divide the flour equally, each student gets 4 cups.

Use counters to find the mean of the data set.

1. 3, 5, 7, 5

Draw 4 stacks to show the data set.

Make the stacks the same height.

_____ counters in each stack.

Mean: _____

2. 5, 7, 4, 3, 4, 1

Draw 6 stacks to show the data set.

Make the stacks the same height.

_____ counters in each stack.

Mean: _____

Statistics and Probability

Mean as Fair Share and Balance Point

Use counters to find the mean of the data set.

1. Six students count the number of buttons on their shirts.
   The students have 0, 4, 5, 2, 3, and 4 buttons.

   Make _____**6**_____ stacks of counters with heights 0, 4, 5, 2, 3, and 4.

   Rearrange the counters so that all _____**6**_____ stacks have the same height.

   After rearranging, every stack has _____**3**_____ counters.

   So, the mean of the data set is _____**3**_____.

2. Four students completed 1, 2, 2, and 3 chin-ups. _____

Make a dot plot for the data set and use it to check whether the given value is a balance point for the data set.

3. Sandy's friends ate 0, 2, 3, 4, 6, 6, and 7 pretzels.
   Sandy says the mean of the data is 4. Is Sandy correct?

   ```
   +--+--+--+--+--+--+--+--+--+--+
   0  1  2  3  4  5  6  7  8  9  10
   ```

The total distance from 4 for values less than 4 is _____.
The total distance from 4 for values greater than 4 is

_____. The mean of 4 _____ a balance point.

So, Sandy _____ correct.

Problem Solving REAL WORLD

4. Three baskets contain 8, 8, and 11 soaps.
   Can the soaps be rearranged so that there
   is an equal whole number of soaps in each
   basket? Explain why or why not.

   _____
   _____
   _____
   _____

5. Five pages contain 6, 6, 9, 10, and 11 stickers.
   Can the stickers be rearranged so that there
   is an equal whole number of stickers on each
   page? Explain why or why not.

   _____
   _____
   _____
   _____

Lesson 99

COMMON CORE STANDARD CC.6.SP.5c

Lesson Objective: Summarize a data set by using mean, median, and mode.

Measures of Center

A **measure of center** is a single value that describes the middle of a data set.

The **mean** is the sum of all items in a set of data divided by the number of items in the set.

The **median** is the middle number or the mean of the middle two numbers when the items in the data set are listed in order.

The **mode** is the data value that is repeated more than other values. A data set can have more than one mode, or no mode.

Find the mean, median, and mode for the set of data.
80, 74, 82, 77, 86, 75

Find the mean.

Step 1 Find the sum of the data.
$80 + 74 + 82 + 77 + 86 + 75 = 474$

Step 2 Count the number of data items.
There are 6 items.

Step 3 Divide.

$$\frac{\text{sum}}{\text{number of items}} = \frac{474}{6} = 79$$

So, the mean is 79.

Find the mode.

Use the ordered list and look for numbers that repeat.
No numbers repeat. So, there is no mode.

Find the median.

Step 1 Order the data.
74, 75, 77, 80, 82, 86

Step 2 Find the middle number.
There are two middle numbers:
77 and 80.

Step 3 Find their mean.

$$\frac{77 + 80}{2} = 78.5$$

So, the median is 78.5.

Find the mean, median, and mode.

1. 31, 3, 14, 31, 11

mean: _____   median: _____

mode: _____

2. 95, 18, 51, 1, 22, 5

mean: _____   median: _____

mode: _____

3. 14, 22, 15, 7, 14, 0, 12

mean: _____   median: _____

mode: _____

4. 67, 103, 94, 65, 18, 114, 94, 63, 94, 27

mean: _____   median: _____

mode: _____

Lesson 99

CC.6.SP.5c

Measures of Center

Use the table for 1–4.

1. What is the mean of the data?

$$\frac{10 + 8 + 11 + 12 + 6}{5} = \frac{47}{5} = 9.4$$

9.4 points

Number of Points Blaine Scored in Five Basketball Games	
Game	Points Scored
1	10
2	8
3	11
4	12
5	6

2. What is the median of the data?

_____

3. What is the mode(s) of the data?

_____

4. Suppose Blaine played a sixth game and scored 10 points during the game. Find the new mean, median, and mode.

_____

_____

Problem Solving REAL WORLD

5. An auto manufacturer wants their line of cars to have a median gas mileage of 25 miles per gallon or higher. The gas mileage for their five models are 23, 25, 26, 29, and 19. Do their cars meet their goal? Explain.

_____

_____

_____

_____

6. A sporting goods store is featuring several new bicycles, priced at $300, $250, $325, $780, and $350. They advertise that the average price of their bicycles is under $400. Is their ad correct? Explain.

_____

_____

_____

_____

Lesson 100

COMMON CORE STANDARD CC.6.SP.5c

Lesson Objective: Describe overall patterns in data, including clusters, peaks, gaps, and symmetry.

Patterns in Data

The histogram shows the number of minutes a caller had to be placed on hold before talking to a representative.

According to the graph, there were 10 people who were on hold for 0 to 4 minutes.

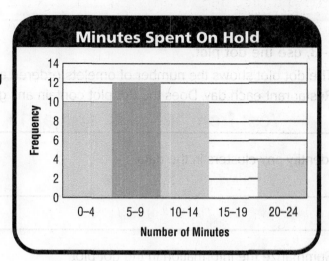

Does the graph contain any clusters or gaps? If so, where? Does the graph have symmetry?

Step 1 Look for a group of data points that lie within a small interval. These are clusters.	The bars for 0–4, 5–9, and 10–14 are in a group. This is a cluster of data.
Step 2 Look for an interval that contains no data. These are gaps.	There is no bar above the interval 15–19. This is a gap in the data. This means there were no people who were on hold for 15 to 19 minutes.
Step 3 Look for symmetry. If you draw a vertical line in the graph, the bars on the left and right sides will match if the graph has symmetry.	A line cannot be drawn anywhere on the graph and have the bars on either side match. There is no symmetry.

Use the dot plot to answer the questions.

1. Are there any clusters? If so, where?

_____

2. Are there any gaps? If so, where?

_____

3. Is there symmetry? If so, where can the line of symmetry be drawn?

_____

Statistics and Probability

Name _____

Patterns in Data

For 1–3, use the dot plot.

1. The dot plot shows the number of omelets ordered at Paul's Restaurant each day. Does the dot plot contain any gaps?

   Yes; from 12 to 13, and at 17

2. Identify any clusters in the data.

   _____

   _____

3. Summarize the information in the dot plot.

   _____

   _____

   _____

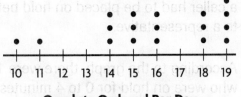

Omelets Ordered Per Day

For 4–5, use the histogram.

4. The histogram shows the number of people that visited a local shop each day in January. How many peaks does the histogram have?

   _____

5. Describe how the data values change across the intervals.

   _____

   _____

   _____

Problem Solving REAL WORLD

6. Look at the dot plot at the right. Does the graph have line symmetry? Explain.

   _____

   _____

   _____

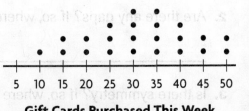

Gift Cards Purchased This Week

Name _____

Lesson **101**

COMMON CORE STANDARD CC.6.SP.5c

Lesson Objective: Understand mean absolute deviation as a measure of variability from the mean.

Mean Absolute Deviation

The **mean absolute deviation** tells how far away the data values are from the mean. A small mean absolute deviation means that most values are close to the mean. A large mean absolute deviation means that the data values are more spread out.

The prices of 8 lunches are $10, $8, $3, $5, $9, $6, $7, and $8.
The mean is $7. Find the mean absolute deviation.

Step 1	Determine how far each data value is from the mean. You can use a number line.	Plot a value on the number line. Then count how many spaces you must move to reach the mean, 7.
		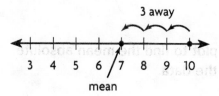

Step 2	Make a list of all of the distances.	Data values: 10 8 3 5 9 6 7 8
		Distance from mean: 3 1 4 2 2 1 0 1

Step 3	Find the mean of the distances by finding the sum and dividing by 8. The quotient is the mean absolute deviation.	$\dfrac{3+1+4+2+2+1+0+1}{8} = \dfrac{14}{8} = 1.75$ So, on average, each data value is 1.75 away from the mean.

Use counters or a number line to find the mean absolute deviation.

1. ages of people on a team in years:
9, 12, 10, 8, 11
mean = 10 years

distances from mean = _____

mean absolute deviation = _____

2. Sam's test scores:
86, 71, 92, 84, 76, 95
mean = 84

mean absolute deviation = _____

3. prices of dinner menu items:
$15, $10, $13, $19, $20, $12, $9, $14
mean = $14

mean absolute deviation = _____

4. daily low temperatures, °F, in a city:
45, 39, 40, 52, 44
mean = 44°F

mean absolute deviation = _____

Mean Absolute Deviation

Use counters and a dot plot to find the mean absolute deviation of the data.

1. the number of hours Maggie spent practicing soccer for 4 different weeks:

   9, 6, 6, 7

   mean = 7 hours

   $$\frac{2 + 1 + 1 + 0}{4} = \frac{4}{4} = 1$$

   mean absolute deviation = _____**1 hour**_____

2. the heights of 7 people in inches:

   60, 64, 58, 60, 70, 71, 65

   mean = 64 inches

   mean absolute deviation = _____

Use the dot plot to find the mean absolute deviation of the data.

3. mean = 10

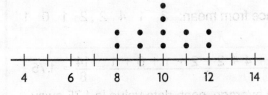

Ages of Students in Dance Class

mean absolute deviation = _____

4. mean = 8

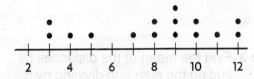

Weekly Hours Spent Doing Homework

mean absolute deviation = _____

Problem Solving REAL WORLD

5. In science class, Troy found the mass, in grams, of 6 samples to be 10, 12, 7, 8, 5, and 6. What is the mean absolute deviation?

   _____

6. Five recorded temperatures are 71°F, 64°F, 72°F, 81°F, and 67°F. What is the mean absolute deviation?

   _____

Name _____

Measures of Variability

Lesson Objective: Summarize a data set by using range, interquartile range, and mean absolute deviation.

A **measure of variability** is a single number that describes how far apart the numbers are in a data set. **Range, interquartile range**, and mean absolute deviation are all measures of variability.

The box plot shows the cost of various concert tickets. Find the range and interquartile range of the data in the box plot.

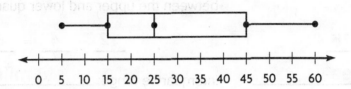

Step 1	To find the range, subtract the least value from the greatest value.	60 − 5 = 55 greatest least range	
Step 2	To find the interquartile range, subtract the lower quartile from the upper quartile.	45 − 15 = 30 upper lower interquartile quartile quartile range	

Make a box plot for the data. Then find the range and interquartile range.

1. number of free throws made:

8, 13, 9, 4, 1, 6, 2, 2, 14, 6, 9, 11

range = _____

interquartile range = _____

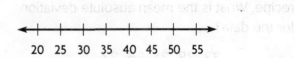

2. minutes spent cooking dinner:
45, 38, 52, 29, 28, 31, 44, 40, 25

range = _____

interquartile range = _____

Statistics and Probability

Measures of Variability

1. Find the range and interquartile range of the data in the box plot.

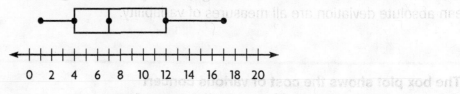

Miles Walked

For the range, find the difference between the greatest and least values.

$$\underline{17} - \underline{1} = \underline{16}$$

range: _____ **16 miles** _____

For the interquartile range, find the difference between the upper and lower quartiles.

$$\underline{12} - \underline{4} = \underline{8}$$

interquartile range: _____ **8 miles** _____

Use the box plot for 2 and 3.

2. What is the range of the data?

_____

3. What is the interquartile range of the data?

_____

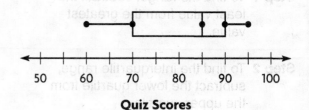

Quiz Scores

Find the mean absolute deviation for the set.

4. heights in centimeters of several flowers:

14, 7, 6, 5, 13

mean absolute deviation: _____

5. ages of several children:

5, 7, 4, 6, 3, 5, 3, 7

mean absolute deviation: _____

Problem Solving

6. The following data set gives the amount of time, in minutes, it took five people to cook a recipe. What is the mean absolute deviation for the data?

33, 38, 31, 36, 37

_____

7. The prices of six food processors are $63, $59, $72, $68, $61, and $67. What is the mean absolute deviation for the data?

_____

Lesson 103

COMMON CORE STANDARD CC.6.SP.5d

Lesson Objective: Determine the effects of
outliers on measures of center and variability.

Effects of Outliers

Sometimes a data set contains a number that is much less or
much greater than the rest. This number is called an **outlier.**
Taking note of outliers can help you understand a data set.

**Use a dot plot to find the outlier for the quiz scores.
Then tell how the outlier affects the mean and median.**

Scores on 20-question Quiz				
15	16	17	13	18
12	5	14	14	16

Mean: 14   Median: 14.5

Step 1 Plot the data on the number line.

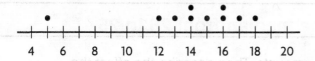

```
    4   6   8   10  12  14  16  18  20
```

Step 2 Find the outlier.   Most of the points are between 12 and 18.
                                       5 is much less than the rest, so it is an outlier.

Step 3 Find the median and mean without the outlier.

Median: Make an ordered list and find the middle value.	Mean: One value has been removed. Add the new list of values and divide by 9.

$$\frac{12 + 13 + 14 + 14 + 15 + 16 + 16 + 17 + 18}{9} = 15$$

12, 13, 14, 14, (15), 16, 16, 17, 18
The new median is 15.   The new mean is 15.

Step 4 Describe the effect of the outlier.
Without the outlier, the mean went up from 14 to 15.
The median went up from 14.5 to 15.

Use the table for Problems 1–3.

1. Find the outlier by drawing a dot plot of the data.

Shirt Prices ($)				
29	33	24	14	29
31	31	33		

Mean: $28   Median: $30

```
    15    18    21    24    27    30    33
```

Outlier: _____

2. Find the mean and median without the outlier.

Median: $ _____   Mean: $ _____

3. Without the outlier, the mean _____.

The median _____.

Statistics and Probability

Effects of Outliers

1. Identify the outlier in the data set of students in each class. Then describe the effect the outlier has on the mean and median.

Students in Each Class				
30	22	26	21	24
28	23	26	28	12

<u>12; Possible answer: The outlier decreases the mean from about 25.3 to 24. The outlier decreases the median from 26 to 25.</u>

2. Identify the outlier in the data set of pledge amounts. Then describe the effect the outlier has on the mean and median.

Pledge Amounts			
$100	$10	$15	$20
$17	$24	$32	$36

_____

_____

3. In a set of points that Milton scored in basketball games, there is an outlier. Before one game, Milton injured his knee. Do you think the outlier is greater or less than the rest of the numbers of points? Explain.

_____

_____

Problem Solving REAL WORLD

4. Duke's science quiz scores are 99, 91, 60, 94, and 95. Describe the effect of the outlier on the mean and median.

_____

_____

_____

5. The number of people who attended an art conference for five days was 42, 27, 35, 39, and 96. Describe the effect of the outlier on the mean and median.

_____

_____

_____

Lesson **104**

COMMON CORE STANDARD CC.6.SP.5d

Lesson Objective: Choose appropriate measures of center and variability to describe data, and justify the choice.

Choose Appropriate Measures of Center and Variability

Sometimes one measure of center or variability represents the data better than another measure of variability. For example, the median might be a better representation than the mean.

Cheeseburger prices at several different restaurants are $5, $3, $2, $6, $4, and $14. Should the mean, median, or mode be used to describe the data? Should the range or interquartile range be used?

Measure of Center	Measure of Variability
Step 1 Find the mean, median, and mode.	**Step 1** Find the range and interquartile range.
Mean: $\dfrac{5 + 3 + 2 + 6 + 4 + 14}{6} \approx \$5.67$	Range: $14 - 2 = \$12$
Median: $2\quad 3\quad 4\,\vert\,5\quad 6\quad 14\quad \dfrac{4 + 5}{2} = \$4.50$	Interquartile range: $6 - 3 = \$3$ $2\ \textcircled{3}\ 4\,\vert\,5\ \textcircled{6}\ 14$
Mode = none	
Step 2 Compare. There are six data values, and the mean is greater than four of them. The outlier of $14 is causing this. So, the median is a better measure of center.	**Step 2** Compare. All of the data values except one are between $2 and $6. The interquartile range is a better measure.

---

1. The times, in minutes, spent cleaning a room are 60, 50, 33, 28, and 44. Decide which measure(s) of center best describes the data set. Explain your reasoning.

_____

_____

_____

_____

2. The amounts of snowfall, in inches, are 4, 3, 20, 6, 8, and 2. Decide which measure(s) of variability best describes the data set. Explain your reasoning.

_____

_____

_____

_____

Choose Appropriate Measures of Center and Variability

1. The distances, in miles, that 6 people travel to get to work are 14, 12, 2, 16, 16, and 18. Decide which measure(s) of center best describes the data set. Explain your reasoning.

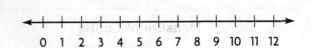

mean = __13 miles__

median = __15 miles__

mode = __16 miles__

The _____ is less than 4 of the data points, and the _____ describes only 2 of the data points. So, the _____ best describes the data.

2. The numbers of pets that several children have are 2, 1, 2, 3, 4, 3, 10, 0, 1, and 0. Make a box plot of the data and find the range and interquartile range. Decide which measure better describes the data set and explain your reasoning.

┤─┼─┼─┼─┼─┼─┼─┼─┼─┼─┼─┼─┼─►
0 1 2 3 4 5 6 7 8 9 10 11 12

range = _____

interquartile range = _____

_____

_____

_____

Problem Solving REAL WORLD

3. Brett's history quiz scores are 84, 78, 92, 90, 85, 91, and 0. Decide which measure(s) of center best describes the data set. Explain your reasoning.

mean = _____ median = _____

mode = _____

_____

_____

_____

4. Eight students were absent the following number of days in a year: 4, 8, 0, 1, 7, 2, 6, and 3. Decide if the range or interquartile range better describes the data set, and explain your reasoning.

range = _____ interquartile range = _____

_____

_____

_____